ELIXIR
Of The Soul

ELIXIR
Of The Soul

Encountering Life's True Remedy

MONICA MARTINEZ

ARPress
ILLUMINATING IDEAS.
EMPOWERING VOICES

ARPress
45 Dan Road Suite 36
Canton MA 02021

Hotline: 1(888) 821-0229
Fax: 1(508) 545-7580

Ordering Information:
Quantity Sales. Special discounts are available on quantity purchases by corporations, associations, and others. For details, contact the publisher at the address above.

Printed in the United States of America.

ISBN-13	Softcover	979-8-89676-507-3
	eBook	979-8-89676-508-0

Library of Congress Control Number: 2024924657

DEDICATION

First and foremost, this book is dedicated to the One True Elohim (God) of my spirit, soul, and body; I must give HIM all the glory and honor for giving me another day to live on this earth and to share His truth with as many as possible. Secondly, I dedicate this tome to the love of my life here in this world, my husband, Pastor Paul Martinez. He is a truly anointed man of Yah, an apostle for such a time is this, full of faith and dedication to God, his family and to the assembly of Greater Faith Church. Oh, how I love this man!!

TABLE OF CONTENTS

INTRODUCTION

The Soul's Quest of Love's Salvation

There is a yearning in the soul of every man with a deep and intense burning for true love escorting the fanatical passion of gratification, a type of salvation per se, with the affectionate concord and contentment that can no one disavow. The soul's powerful emotion of desire drives this obsessive being on a quest to search for the treasure that will deliver true fulfilment. He longs for an elixir, a remedy or even a cure to his hungry and craving soul; it is as if something key is missing to a dreadful desolate fragment of the inner being. Without this piece of the puzzle to complete him, the diligent hunt becomes an addiction to soothe his yawning desire for the drug to tame his emerging rage. He believes the robust sentiment of love will fix his down- cast infirmity, hence wayfaring towards love's therapy to obtain the elixir of love. The poet strongly conveys this aspect in the lyrical text of a stirring love story[1] between two lovers as both express their powerful appetite towards each other as one writes, *"By night on my bed I sought him whom my **soul loveth**: I sought him, but I found him not. I will rise now, and go about the city in the streets, and in the broad ways I will seek him whom my **soul** loveth: **I sought him**, but I found him not. The watchmen that go about the city found me: to whom I said, Saw ye him whom my soul loveth? It was but a little that I passed from them, but I found him whom my soul loveth: I held him, and would not let him go, until I had brought*

---

[1] The author to this poetic book is accredited to third and richest king to rule over Israel, King Solomon, the son of King David. He tells of the romance between a bride and groom who experience a longing and discontentment without each other.

him into my mother's house, and into the chamber of her that conceived me" (Song of Solomon 3:1-4, KJV).

Where does one begin to look for that remedy, he longs for to appease the pain in his soul? This is not a quest for a treasure of gold, silver or money; but it is for a genuine pearl of true peace and contentment that no money could purchase. It is for a downcast soul that cries out for comfort, who runs to and fro searching for an answer to his ailment. It is not an infirmity of the body itself, but a discontentment of the soul—the mind, will and emotions. Could the "robust sentiment of love" truly be the answer to the love sick soul?

The Atmosphere of the Starving Soul

The atmosphere is dark and dim for the one who starves and moans for the formula of true salvation that can convey love to his soul. He holds on to hope with an assurance in a rescuer that could assist in discovering that penetrating sentiment of a love like no other. It is the type of love that could fill the heart with passion and escort fulfillment, hope, and peace of mind. This expectation of a liberator with the power of true love floods his mind in dream and thought; it is that cure that could possibly raise his lowly and heavy heart to a restful delight.

The disgruntled ingenuity battles within while becoming disconsolate and isolated in his negated shamble. This appalling individual who has found no cure or repair becomes anxious, fearful and paranoid, looking at others, wishing to obtain what they possess. The desperation and need for serenity become so great that the hysteria of thoughts converts to displeasure in temperament displaying extreme and outrageous demeanors. Harmony and calmness are now remote and unattainable to the heavy soul that screams out for true love, compassion, healing and security. Prolonging clashes in the thoughts of this oppressed individual now cause him to lose the will to live; he finds no reparation for his hurting heart. He continues to ask, "Where lays the answer to the grievous soul?"

The Missing Antidote for the Soul

Where does one go for that solution which will supply the antidote or elixir for the soul? In the world today there are numerous "fulfillment" remedies for the perplexed, but the necessity for contentment continues to grow at an unbelievable rate in the lives of many. The existence of copious agents of psychiatric wards, psychological facilities, counseling/therapy entities and spiritual healing centers proves this precise point; man needs help in his soul. There is such a need for contentment accompanying healing, and the desire to experience pleasure with true gratification is outrageous. These establishments in operation indicate they have no difficulty filling doctor's offices with patients who want to vent their problematic passions. The disappointing facts prove these services show no change to make lives better or in positively aiding people with authentic essentials for the soul. They neither provide the genuine preferred outcome nor do any deliver long-term therapeutic healing; and "interventions" remain null and void. While bank accounts of these "educated certified doctors and therapists" grow in surplus, the numerous hurting souls lose all hope, and the continual suffusing of morgues exhibit no deficit. Band-Aids of sedatives, therapy sessions, and mental wards are not the cure-all for depression or oppression; in addition, while anti-depressants soar off pharmacy shelves, they have neither been found a nostrum or restorative agent to the frustrated or miserable soul.

Could the answer possibly be found in faith or a "Higher Power"—a power even greater than all other creeds and gods, but not yet revealed to the soul of man? The question is, "Who is that very One that is able to deliver an answer, Who will save the soul from destruction?" Could this Higher Power perhaps be the answer to life's most difficult questions regarding love and the salvation of the soul? How about His love towards humanity; will His answer lead to the truth? What shall then be done with all other religions and their "sacred gods" and the writings or tomes of their followers of significance which numerous personalities take to heart by living the lifestyle of the author or guru? Or, shall one lean toward the attitude of Christopher Hitchens, author of the book, God is not Great, (New York, NY: Twelve Publishing, 2007), pp. 5-6, where he states that a good and virtuous life can be lived without religion. Should the longing soul perhaps not waste time in seeking the answer in religion or a god at all? He writes:

> "We are reconciled to living only once, except through our children, for whom we are perfectly happy to notice that we must make way, and room. We speculate that it is at

least possible that, once people accepted the fact of their short and struggling lives, they might behave better toward each other and not worse. We believe with certainty that an ethical life can be lived without religion. And we know for a fact that the corollary holds true—that religion has caused innumerable people not just to conduct themselves no better than others, but to award themselves permission to behave in ways that would make a brothel-keeper or an ethnic cleaner raise an eyebrow."

According to the writer of Psalms 42:1-11, he believes he has found the antidote to his panting soul, which is cast down, in God. He believes that if he remembers God, that He will command His loving kindness towards him and thus help him to regain his sanity. He believes that God will bring him hope and health to his countenance as God brings him back to a place where he once experienced love and its benefits. He[2] states: *"As the hart panteth after the water brooks, so panteth **my soul after thee, O God**. My **soul thirsteth** for God, for the living God: when shall I come and appear before God? My tears have been my meat day and night, while they continually say unto me, Where is thy God? When I remember these things, I pour out my soul in me: for I had gone with the multitude, I went with them to the house of God, with the voice of joy and praise, with a multitude that kept holyday. Why art thou cast down, O my soul? and why art thou disquieted in me? hope thou in God: for I shall yet praise him for the help of his countenance. O my God, my soul is cast down within me: therefore will I remember thee from the land of Jordan, and of the Hermonites, from the hill Mizar. Deep calleth unto deep at the noise of thy waterspouts: all thy waves and thy billows are gone over me. Yet the LORD will command his lovingkindness in the daytime, and in the night his song shall be with me, and my prayer unto the God of my life. I will say unto God my rock, Why hast thou forgotten me? why go I mourning because of the oppression of the enemy? As with a sword in my*

---

[2]   The Psalmist of this lamenting poem was in exile far from the temple. This Psalm is attributed to the sons of Korah, a musical family in Israel who were descendants from the priest who led a rebellion against Moses and Aaron found in Numbers 16. The judgment of God came upon Korah and his acquaintances, but Korah's family continued for hundreds of years to lead the worship in Israel.

bones, mine enemies reproach me; while they say daily unto me, Where is thy God? Why art thou cast down, O my soul? and why art thou disquieted within me? hope thou in God: for I shall yet praise him, who is the health of my countenance, and my God" (KJV).

The Apostle John declares of a true love that is so powerful towards humanity that it is able to save the vile soul from perishing[3]. It is a genuine love not of this world and neither to be found in man's soul; only in the spirit of man can it be dispersed. It is a unique love originating in the heavenlies; it is the *Most Genuine Love of all,* Who likewise is on His own expedition with the intention to reconcile Himself with His own. The chaser, now becomes the chased by Love Himself; He is relentless in collecting back to Himself His own treasure; what once was lost, now could be found through the most perfect and flawless Savior. Many say, "He is the Answer above all man-made elixirs or tonics; He is the innocent lamb without spot, wrinkle or blemish, sacrificing His own life for the very ones fashioned as He." The most farfetched statement of all is "We were known by Him before the foundations of the world." Could this truly be the missing formula to man's infirmity of the soul? Is He truly the healing remedy-Savior, given by God, because of His everlasting love? What "love" is this with the "Name" above all names that can save the lost and dying world?

For this reason, as shown above, we seek diligently for the "Elixir for the soul." The world is full of souls existing in confusion and seeking a way of redemption while craving after that missing element to comfort and satisfy their famine state. Coveting appeasement to their ailment, they scatter to and fro looking for that extraordinary jewel to convey a salvation. While there are psychologists, psychoanalysts, drug therapies, spiritual remedies and all other types of treatment plans to assist in comforting the sick ambiance, man remains the same in his limbo state of wishful thinking. The same pain with the aching heart remains broken and answerless; the road seems a never-ending one. The great wanderer, maundering about to find the missing element to the tonic for the lethargic and disconcerting soul, begins his voyage.

---

[3] This passage is written by the same writer, the Apostle John. He states, *"For God so loved the world, that he gave his only begotten Son, that whosoever believeth in him should not perish, but have everlasting life"* (John 3:16, KJV).

Because of so many "treatments," the depths of this inaccessible personality is gloomy which imprisons him into a seemingly never-ending bottomless pit, grasping for a glimmer of breath, longing for an inhalation or exhalation of some kind of liberation. Could the answer be found in a certain religion that connects man to the spiritual world? Or, could life truly be great without religion or relief from a Higher Power like God?

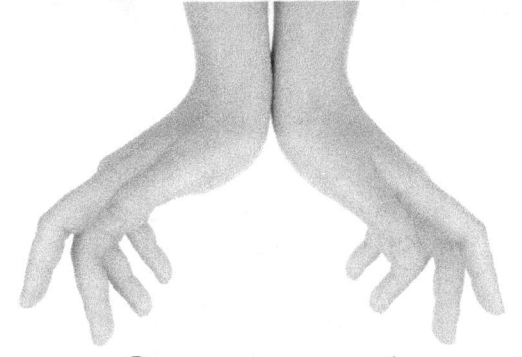

CHAPTER 1

Understanding the Spirit, Soul and Body Connection

F irst and foremost, the meaning of the word "soul" must be clear in order to comprehend the valid meaning of "the yearning soul of man." To the reader, the soul and spirit may represent the same thing, but distinguishing between the two is essential to understand the root of the "longing," or the origin of the nostalgia he is experiencing. The melancholia derives from either the soul or the spirit, and both are debatable. Man has both a spirit and a soul and lives in a body. Both "saved[4]" and "unsaved," or what others call "believers" or "unbelievers" of God, still have a spirit, soul and body. The difference is that the unsaved person, or non-believer in Christ, does not have the Spirit of God living in his own spirit and thus, is unable to have communion with God. This is also known as having a "born again" experience with God, having the spirit part of man re-born and reconciled with God. Before receiving Jesus in the heart of man, the soul and spirit are lost; in other words, this person is dead spiritually because God moved out when Adam ate of the forbidden fruit[5]. Because of Adam's

---

4   To be "saved" means to accept Jesus Christ, the Son of God in one's heart; according to the Apostle Paul's writing, he states: "*That if thou shalt confess with thy mouth the Lord Jesus, and shalt believe in thine heart that God hath raised him from the dead, thou shalt be saved*" (Romans 10:9, KJV).

5   The account of this disobedience towards God is found in Genesis 3 of the Holy Bible.

disobedience, due to his free will, his soul over-ruled, he lost that connection with God, and in the process died spiritually[6]. Unless he believes and receives Jesus Christ the Son of God as his personal Savior in his heart, man cannot again experience that intimate relationship with God which was lost in the Garden of Eden.

At times the Bible refers to man's soul as functioning no differently from man's spirit[7] in an unsaved or unregenerate state; this is because his soul over-rules and greatly influences his spirit, consequently manifesting the works or behaviors of the soul. Sadly, this one cannot differentiate between his own spirit and soul. According to the Bible, man is made in the image and likeness of his Creator, the True and Living "God" (Elohim[8]). Like his Maker, God the Father, God the Son and God the Holy Spirit, Who are known as the Trinity, man is made as a three-dimensional being having a spirit, soul and a body. In the first chapter in Genesis, God's initial words concerning the whole man reads as, *"And God said, Let **us** make man in **our** image, after our likeness: and let them have **dominion** over the fish of the sea, and over the fowl of the air, and over the cattle, and over all the earth, and over every creeping thing that creepeth upon the earth. So God created man in his own image, in the image of God created he him; male and female created he them"* (Genesis 1:26-27, KJV).

God's formula to man entire is found in Genesis 2:7 which states, *"And the* LORD *God formed man of the dust of the ground, and breathed into his nostrils the breath of life; and man became a living soul"* (KJV).

---

[6] Genesis 2:16-17 states, *"And the* LORD *God commanded the man, saying, Of every tree of the garden thou mayest freely eat: But of the tree of the knowledge of good and evil, thou shalt not eat of it: for in the day that thou eatest thereof thou shalt surely die"* (KJV).

[7] Watchman Nee, in his book, The Spiritual Man, (New York, NY: Christian Fellowship Publishers, Inc. 1968), p. 35, states, "In searching the Scriptures it does seem that an unregenerated spirit functions no differently from the way the soul does." The Biblical references he uses are found in: Genesis 41:8; Judges 8:3 Darby; Proverbs 14:29 Darby; Proverbs 17:22; Isaiah 29:24; Isaiah 65:14; Daniel 5:20.

[8] Elohim is the name for "God" in the opening chapter of Genesis. W. G. Plaut, editor of The Torah (New York, NY: By the Union of American Hebrew Congregation, 1981) p. 31, states that in chapter 2 God is called Adonai Elohim in which, *"Jewish tradition interprets the names Elohim and Adonai as explanations of the two sides of the nature of God, the former representing the quality of justice, the latter reflecting the quality of mercy."*

Consequently, the body by itself was the materials of earth, dust and soil with the perfect pattern of God Himself, and then God breathed[9] into man's nostrils His own breath of life[10] giving man his spirit, then man became a soul,[11] a breathing creature. Watchman Nee, author of the book, The Latent Power of the Soul, (New York, NY: Christian Fellowship Publishers, Inc. 1972) pp. 10-11, describes the trilogy of spirit, soul and body. He states:

> "'And Jehovah God formed man of the dust of the ground' (Gen. 2.7). This refers to the human body. 'And breathed into his nostrils the breath of life.' This describes how God gave spirit to man; it was Adam's spirit. So man's body was formed of the dust of the ground, and man's spirit was given to him by God. 'And man became a living soul.' After the breath of life had entered into his nostrils man became a living soul. The spirit, the soul, and the body are three separate entities. 'May your spirit and soul and body be preserved entire' (I Thess. 5:23). The spirit is God-given; the soul is a living soul; and the body is God-formed.
>
> According to common understanding the soul is our personality. When the spirit and the body were joined, man became a living soul. The characteristic of the angels is spirit and that of the lower animals such as beasts is flesh. We humans have both spirit and body; but our characteristic is neither spirit nor body but soul. We have a living soul. Hence the Bible calls man soul. For example, when Jacob went down into Egypt with his family, the Scriptures tell us that 'all the souls of the house of Jacob, that came into Egypt, were threescore and ten' (Gen. 46.27). Again, those who had received Peter's word on Pentecost were baptized and 'there were added unto them in that day about three thousand souls' (Acts 2.41). Hence soul stands for our personality, for what makes us as man."

---

[9] The word "breathed" in Greek is "*Pneuma,*" which means "spirit."

[10] The word "life" in the Greek is "*Psuche,*" which means "soul."

[11] The word "soul" in the Greek is "*Nephash,*" meaning "a breathing creature."

The discussion in controversy is geared towards the "soul," the part of man that is appalling, and therefore covets soothing. The soul realm of man is likewise three dimensions, comprised of the mind, will and emotions; these are the parts where man thinks (mind), where he makes choices (will), and has feelings (emotions). Hence, when referring to the "soul" of man, it is in the area of his thoughts and his belief system, the place where everyday living begins which *will* determine the choices he makes. The choices he makes will determine his feelings: anger, sadness, bitterness, loneliness, joyfulness, peacefulness, contentment or happiness; all three factors will now govern his totality. Man's soul will either manifest behaviors of displeasure and dissatisfaction, or he will manifest actions of peace and contentment. Thus, the "yearning soul" is the mislaid soul who lacks harmony and satisfaction in his life and seeks to fill the empty part, hoping to provide that lost piece of fulfillment for which he pines. Man's soul links with his own spirit at one end and links with his body at the other end; in other words, the soul is the middle man having access to his spirit and his body. Since God is the Creator of man's entire make-up, there must be a God link and explanation to why man's soul becomes wretched. Andrew Murray, writer of the book, <u>The Spirit of Christ</u>, (Fort Washington, PA: Christian Literature Crusade, 1964, Note C: The Place of the Indwelling) pp. 227-228, gives his explanation of the triune dimensions of man. He says:

> "In the history of man's creation we read, 'The Lord God formed man of the dust of the ground'—thus was his body made—'and breathed into his nostrils the breath' or spirit 'of life': thus his spirit came from God; 'and man became a living soul.' The spirit quickening the body made man a living soul, a living person with the consciousness of himself. The soul was the meeting-place, the point of union between body and spirit. Through the body, man, the living soul, stood related to the external world of sense; could influence it, or be influenced by it. Through the spirit he stood related to the spiritual world and the Spirit of God, whence he had his origin; could be the recipient and the minister of its life and power. Standing thus midway between two worlds, belonging to both, the soul had the power of determining

itself, of choosing or refusing the objects by which it was surrounded, and to which it stood related.

In the constitution of these three parts of man's nature, the spirit, as linking him with the Divine, was the highest; the body, connecting him with the sensible and animal, the lowest; intermediate stood the soul, partaker of the nature of the others, the bond on each other. Its work, as the central power, was to maintain them in their due relation; to keep the body, as the lowest, in subjection to the spirit; itself to receive through the spirit, as the higher, from the Divine Spirit what was waiting (sic) it for its perfection: and so to pass down, even to the body, that by which it might be partaker of the Spirit's perfection and become a spiritual body."

C. I. Scofield, in his reference Bible, gives a clear explanation about consciousness, He states, "the spirit gives God-consciousness, the soul self-consciousness, the body world-consciousness. Horse and ox are not conscious of God because they have no spirit. They are only conscious of their own beings. The body causes us to sense the world—such as our seeing the things of the world, our feeling hot or cold, and so forth." Accordingly, the soul is the self-conscious region where self-mental disorders and appetites constitute factors of emotional sufferings.

Nowadays when "emotional distresses" or "emotional sufferings" are mentioned, many are quick to reference those as emotionally unstable or mentally disturbed. They will swiftly suggest that perhaps these mental issues can be resolved with psychiatry or psychology. They will refer to the pain of man as an illness or disease in the mind and blame the cause on a chemical imbalance or upbringing. In addition, they will not initiate to state or even believe that man's make-up is triune in the likeness of the "Ultimate Creator—God." Lester Sumrall, author of the book, Spirit Soul & Body, (New Kensington, PA: Whitaker House, 1984), pp. 11-12, states that psychiatry, psychology, and philosophy teach that man's composite is a two-part creature. He states:

"Outside of the Bible, man is a dualism or two-part creature. Psychiatry, psychology, and philosophy teach that man is two parts. They think he is inside and outside, topside and bottomside. The Word of God says that man is three.

I really feel that God is doing a new thing on the earth today in a remarkable and wonderful way. God is exploding revelation in this end time. This truth has not been fully taught in our generation.

Historical Truth and Pertinent Truth
There are two embodiments of truth. One of these truths is historical truth, and the other is pertinent truth. We should have a thorough comprehension of this.

Historical truth is unrelated to your destiny. For example, once there was a man named Noah who built a big boat. Noah was not a shipbuilder, but God gave him the blueprints and taught him how to build it. Until 1850 A.D., nobody ever built a boat as big as his. We accept this story as history, but it has nothing to do with the peace that is in our hearts now. It has nothing to do with the joy that is in our soul. It is true, but it is historical truth.

Pertinent truth is the opposite of that. It has to do with the fact that God loves you, He gave His Son for you, and you can be saved forever right now!

There are literally worlds of *pertinent truth* in the Bible. They have to do with your joy, happiness, and peace. The doctrine of the total man belongs in the column of pertinent truth. You must understand yourself to be a successful Christian. You have to know who you are before you can direct yourself to be a successful Christian. You have to know who you are before you can direct yourself. It is possible that 95 percent of all the Christians in our land (even though they are born again and their spirits are alive) still live, act, and think in their Adamic nature. They are living in the old man. Within them abides the secret of the new man, but they have not been taught pertinent truth; they are living in the ways and the feelings of the old Adamic nature. God is now calling them to a new life in Christ Jesus. This is why I want to lead you into the exploration of the third great area of truth: the understanding of ourselves—the total man."

In addition, these behavior scientists will neither claim nor believe there is some kind of God-link in the creation of man. They insist on relying upon science and only accept as true what can be proven by experiment; this remains their view. In the minds of these, even to believe in the existence of a supernatural realm or that man's composite is part soul is absurd. Keith S. Cornish[12], an atheist with the *Atheist Foundation of Australia Inc.,* gives his perspective on the spirit realm and on the "soul." He states:

> "The simple fact is that all life-forms end in death and the elements of which they are composed return to the air and the earth to be taken up and recycled in some new organism.
>
> This natural process is universal and is beyond dispute. What is challenged by atheists and freethinkers is the claim made by purveyors of religion that humans alone of all living forms have a 'soul' or 'spirit' which survives death and carries the essential characteristics of the person to a supernatural existence in a supernatural realm.
>
> The method or pathway for making this crossing to a new life beyond the grave varies widely between religions and between the multitude of Christian denominations. The Roman Catholic Church is probably the most dogmatic in its proclaimed route to Paradise – infant christening, confirmation, frequent mass attendances and the final rites. Donations and prayers to the saints are desirable adjuncts guarding against a period in purgatory.
>
> Atheists maintain that the concept of humankind having a unique supernatural 'soul' is simply a primitive notion which has no basis in fact and that religious organizations are guilty of perpetrating a colossal fraud on ignorant and gullible people, chiefly through the indoctrination of infants. They are aided and abetted by the media who fear adverse reaction affecting profits if the facts are revealed.
>
> On what grounds can atheists make the claim that no-one has a supernatural 'soul'?

---

[12] This quote retrieved from the article "An Atheist's Perspective on Death" by Keith S. Cornish, Past President of the *Atheist Foundation of Australia* Inc., from 1975-2005, (website: http://ateistfoundation.org.au/).

There is no scientific evidence of anything super-natural. There is no credible evidence that humankind is a unique creation by a deity. There is no credible definition of a 'soul.'

Scientific evidence completely destroys all the concepts which are the basis for the existence of the 'soul.'"

In spite of all explanations of atheists and scientific intellectuals who believe they have all the right questions and answers to crush the indication of a triune man because of a triune God, they still do not have an answer to the foreboding soul. They too have been known to be lost and come to realize that their theories have been nothing more than a bag of kitty litter. It was Ralph Waldo Emerson[13] who said, "All I have seen teaches me to trust the Creator for all I have not seen." It was the celebrated and brilliant writer, C.S. Lewis who stated, "If I find in myself desires which nothing in this world can satisfy, the only logical explanation is that I was made for another world." Isaac Newton had his own words to share as he stated, "I seem to have been only a boy playing on the sea-shore, and diverting myself in now and then finding a smoother pebble or a prettier shell than ordinary, whilst the great ocean of truth lay all undiscovered before me." In addition, the famous rocket scientist, Wernher von Braun, whose crowning achievement as head of NASA's Marshall Space Flight Center, and leader of the development of the Saturn V booster rocket that aided the landing of the first men on the Moon in 1969 of July, was considered to be "a self-righteous, self-absorbed atheist" who became a believer while seeking the truth. He states, "After receiving my Masters of Science degree in Aerospace Engineering systems design, I was still seeking the truth. No longer a self-admitted atheist, I was just an intellectually honest seeker of the truth. The Designer and Creator of everything did it all for a reason. The splendor of creation and the purpose of man were designed to bring glory and honor to their Creator." Braun also stated, "Scientific concepts exist only in the minds of men. Behind

---

[13] Usage of quotes taken from Ray Comfort's book, <u>How to know God Exists</u>, (Alachua, Florida: Bridge-Logos, 2007) pp. 19, 81, 155 and 163. Ralph Waldo Emerson, C. S. Lewis, Isaac Newton, and Wernher von Braun were among the many intellectuals who searched for the truth regarding the existence of God.

these concepts lies the reality, which is being revealed to us, but only by the grace of God." What all these famous men had in common was their intelligence; these brilliant minds that once gave the impression that they were masters of their own universe were humbled by realizing they did not have all the answers. How ironic that they too found themselves lost, and it did not matter how knowledgeable they were or how many degrees hung on their wall.

In writing to the Corinthians, the Apostle Paul knew firsthand what mere knowledge could do to the character of man. He too was a man of intelligence who was taught and trained by the prominent Gamaliel to become a Rabbi. He states, *"Now about food offered to idols: of course, we know that all of us possess knowledge [concerning these matters.* **Yet mere] knowledge causes people to be puffed up (to bear themselves loftily and be proud), but love (affection and goodwill and benevolence) edifies and builds up and encourages one to grow [to his full stature]"** (I Corinthians 8:1, AMP).

In essence, the fact remains that the "yearning soul" lost in confusion desires to know the full truth. Looking for what is relied on by one's own achievements to fill the huge void in life, the continuance of dead ends never seems to expire. Man's already disgruntled state of mind proves the fact that he has become corrupt with self; he is his own greatest enemy who allows his soul to rule and dictate the pathway to his fate. Yes, God has given to every man a soul, and he has the power to choose for himself how to live and how to love; because God first loved mankind from the beginning of time, it was never meant for man to live a life full of defeat; on the contrary, he was meant to have dominion over the earth, and to live a life of delight and pleasure. The refusal to obey and the belief that it was more necessary to please himself rather than the One Who created him, Who gave him the world, literally, caused man to lose all the blessings of his Father. It was never meant for the soul of His perfectly knit human beings to "yearn" or to "lack" anything; it was meant for His own to live as kings and priests with dominion over the earth, to replenish and subdue it and to enjoy life to the fullest. Because of one man's disobedience, man became a love sick vessel of the mind, will and emotions, not to pour out, but rather to consume all he could to quench his own self-seeking thirsty "yearning of the soul."

CHAPTER 2

Love Sick: The Soul's Need for Love

From the moment of conception, the soul of man longs for a gratification and is born with the need to satisfy his cravings for affection. It is evident as the baby springs out of the birth canal, full of rage, and crying for that attention he desires. Love is the passion for which this newborn infant hungers, aiming towards all the other benefits it emanates—security, comfort, warmth, protection, and yes, the breast milk of mother. This seconds-old being, crying and screaming, is already cussing and cursing in baby language, "Soothe me, carry me, touch me, embrace me and love me," and demands, "Feed me your milk, NOW!" This infant adamantly cries, expecting to receive all his pleas from his significant other, of course, his mother.

Lovesickness from the Beginning

As the child grows, the demands of love are more obvious and the awareness of kindled temper tantrums has become the norm. Becoming knowledgeable of the ostensible parent giving in and bountifully handing over his every desire, the child continues to conduct himself in ways that trigger the very response he craves. As time energizes different changes in the body, his appetite for a deeper and genuine contentment cultivates hunger pains in his soul; his physical hunger is no longer his essential need nor does the satisfaction derived from his mother bring him true fulfillment. He no longer fixates his desire upon the breast milk of his mother; his craving, which at one point brought him a soothing and filling to his little soul, now weans and then gleans towards another.

The need now develops into a different *kind of love* which consumes his thought life; this love he searches for is one that his mother can no longer deliver, and it is a love that at times he cannot express in words. At times he finds himself resentful towards his own mother, at the fact that what he burns for, she cannot give him. The emptiness of his soul is what man may call, the "magical elixir of the soul," the missing ingredient which is sought to bring a soothing and healing; it is now a matter of embarking on a quest to find that remedy that will calm the colic soul of that urge.

Though he thought he may have found love, the tonic to soothe his ailing romanticism, he finds no fulfillment; his famished soul continues to be in want, and he is not yet complete. He finds himself in a discontent habitation of solitude, confusion, insecurity and meagerness. He assumes completeness with wife, children, friends, career and an extra love affair, but to no avail; there is no sovereignty to his insolvent state. He exists in a poverty of the soul, a need to fill the void depths of his inner parts; he groans for unfeigned gratification. The mislaid soul searches for that salvation in other antidotes to sooth the heartache that wounds his somber grief-stricken state to the core part of his totality. What love's salvation is this?

Addiction to Love for Survival

There is a truth that no one can deny; it is the profound truth that the greatest need for every person is a salvation escorting true love to the soul. From the moment of conception in the womb of a mother, the developing baby needs a savior providing love and attention with the proper nutrients that are imperative in assisting the infant to fully mature. It is essential that the mother take the necessary vitamins and minerals throughout the stages of pregnancy in order for the developing baby to grow properly and healthy. It is a fact that the growing baby in the womb can hear the voice of a loving and compassionate mother's voice and recognizes that same tender vocal sound as he enters the world. As soon as the baby senses the mother's presence in the room, the cry of aspiration for the warmth and embrace of its mother's breast is sought after. The love permeates throughout the room between mother and baby and the bond becomes stronger as the feeding baby lays upon her chest. All the pain this mother endures during her many hours of labor vanishes in the sweet loving presence of her new-born baby.

On the other hand, if the baby is not properly taken care of and given the proper nourishment while in the developing stages of pregnancy, the infant could possibly be born with birth defects. This baby senses not love, but the turmoil and stress of the mother who fails to pay attention to the new life in her womb. She constantly speaks negatively about the pregnancy and wishes this had never happened. The baby never hears the gentle voice of a caring mother; instead of a kind and loving sound, he only hears the yelling of a stressful and dysfunctional family who did not care nor anticipate the arrival of a new life into the world. The uncaring mother seeks the opportunity for an abortion but finds it is too late in the pregnancy for that option. She decides not to take the advice of the physician whom her case worker advises her to see; rather, she decides to continue in her drug addiction and to visit the crack house down the street which supplies her with drugs weekly. Because of the heavy amount of cocaine in her system and the neglecting of her pregnancy, the underweight and sickly baby prematurely arrives. As soon as this infant is born, the only hands he feels are the slimy latex gloves worn by the nurse practitioner who carries his little frail body to the closest incubator holding oxygen over his tiny nose and mouth. This baby belongs to no joyful mother who is warming, compassionate or loving, but rather is a possession of the state of Texas, who has been rendered a drug addict at birth. His cry is not for the loving tender voice of a mother and her breast milk, but rather his cries are for the formula mixture of cocaine to soothe his drug addiction craving. This is a love sick baby.

Both babies in this illustration have a need for a savior to deliver the security of safety in the wrapping arms of a loving mother. Both have a need to receive love and to give love, but only one receives these gifts at birth. Although neither infant has the choice of whether they receive that security or not, one still lacks that very essential need for love. However, as both babies grow into maturity, still the need for the salvation of their souls is essential. They both find that it is no longer the protection of an affectionate mother that they need; it is now something deeper in the soul that is missing. This missing component, they do not know yet, but must search for that absent piece of the puzzle that completes them.

One may think that because one infant was born to a home of security and love that there would be no problem with a need for his soul when he has grown, but this is a sad mistake; or, because the other infant was born a drug addict and given to the state perhaps this one would definitely have a greater need of salvation in his soul to love; again, this is sad mistake. Regardless of how each infant was born or the kind of environment they inhabit, both will grow and still have a need for a deeper security and a deeper love that will satisfy the soul part of their being, for as both mature, both will have a need for the salvation of his soul.

This salvation they both seek will be the missing factor which conveys the very essentials that were needed as infants, but to a much greater degree. They will both find, when they come to the age of accountability, that a mother, wife, family, career or extra-marital affair will not mend or rectify the nostalgia of the soul. Both will grow with a form of love sickness of the soul longing for completeness and fulfillment. Both will long for true satisfaction, but neither will find what they seek for in any worldly possession or in any person; they will arrive at a fork in the road wondering which way to go or where to look for that very answer to the missing piece. It is the fragment to their disoriented soul that binds them to an aching heart that is unexplainable to any other; it is a feeling that both believe no one else has ever, or will ever, experience. Of course, it is only a belief that each one has, for every soul of man arrives at a point in their life to find out that the greatest need in life is a definite love like no other.

At some point in time, each will individually discover that something is absent from the entirety of their soul which displeases them; they are truly unhappy and long for a pleasure that words cannot express. They soon find themselves in the same old pattern of life, looking for a love that will please their lost soul, believing that love in a relationship once again is the answer to heal the sympathy of a split heart. Leo F. Buscaglia, Ph.D., author of the book, Loving Each Other, (Fawcett Columbine, NY: Ballantine Books, 1984), pp. 24-25, believes that without relationship there is no being or becoming. He believes that man's survival depends upon relationships of love. He states,

"There is no being or becoming without relationship. From the beginning, we grow to sense the need and import of relatedness. We human beings have the longest period of dependency of any living creature. At birth, in total helplessness, we engage in our first coupling, mother-child, and from that time on, the more sophisticated our lives become, the more interrelated we become. In a sense, we spend our entire existence weaving one relationship into another until we've created, like the web of a spider, a complete pattern.

Our very survival seems to depend upon our relationships. In childhood, if we are denied loving encounters with human beings, we wither, fall into psychosis, idiocy, or die. As adults we continue to depend upon our interactions in togetherness for our greater joys and our most significant growth. We take this process for granted. It seems to be only in moments when we experience disconnection, times when we are severed from close relationships—either by death, divorce, or physical separations that tear our closeness apart and leave us alone—that it becomes apparent. It is strange, then, that even knowing of our desperate need for relating, we continue through much of our lives to engage in thoughtless, vacuous behavior which only results in isolating us further."

The Characteristics of Mania Love

What is described above is the most definite need for love, though he only calls it "relationship." Although it may be true that survival seems to depend upon relationships, the fact of the matter is that this type of love in a relationship will not cause man to have that true inner peace he desires. On the contrary, though these relationships bring joy, they most certainly bring turmoil. What it comes down to is that this particular "love in a relationship" is about pleasing self. Man is a taker of love and receives all the benefits with which it comes. This "survival" that is described above is not at all about giving but about receiving in order to survive. The interactions that cause each to grow depending on the greater joys of life must be consistent. What about when times are not about the "greater joys of life?" What then? Is man unable to grow and survive at all if these relationships are inactive? Many have heard the saying, "I can't live without you." When times of unexpected break-ups occur because one person has "fallen out of love" and no longer likes the situation they find themselves in, getting up and leaving is no problem. But to the other person involved, it is a tragedy. The hurt becomes unbearable at times and when this occurs, this is when man transforms into another persona. As mentioned earlier, because the soul of man needs love, they become "love sick." In an article by Frank Tallis, *"Crazy for You,"* The Psychologist 18, No. 2 (February 2005): 72-74, he asks whether psychologists should take lovesickness more seriously. He writes:

> "Truly, madly, deeply. If you haven't actually said those words, you've probably thought them—and they are very revealing. They suggest that, as a society, we consider 'madness' to be as significant an indicator of love's authenticity as honesty and depth. We do not expect love to be rational – we expect it to be overwhelming, improvident and unpredictable. We expect to 'go crazy'.
>
> The similarities between passionate love and mental illness have been noted since classical times. The ancient Greeks employed the term *theia mania* (or madness from the gods) to describe the sudden overthrow of reason associated with falling in love, and the principles of Hippocratic medicine provide a mechanism that explains why lovers are prone to emotional distress. According to the humoural model, if love becomes too 'heated', vital fluids evaporate creating a cold, dry state known as love melancholy (Babb, 1951; Burton, 1621/2001). The symptoms of love melancholy (or lovesickness) have been celebrated by poets and songwriters from classical times to the present day.
>
> Although we now associate lovesickness with adolescent crushes and romantic fiction, it is in fact one of the most successful of all psychiatric diagnoses. Lovesickness was used by doctors for nearly two thousand years (compared with current ICD-10 or DSM-IV diagnoses, most of

which are less than a hundred years old). It wasn't until the collapse of the humoural model in the 18th century that the diagnosis finally fell out of favour among medical practitioners (see Porter, 2002).

The idea that love is somehow a close cousin of mental illness was never decisively rejected, and it resurfaced again in the work of many contemporary psychologists. Indeed, most extant typologies of love, theories of love and descriptions of love acknowledge at least one feature or mechanism that might be described as 'psychopathological'. Think for example of John Lee's (1973) mania, Dorothy Tennov's (1979) limerence and Robert Sternberg's (1986) infatuation, all of which are characterized by obsession, irrational idealization, emotional instability or emotional dependency."

It is important to realize, that the goal of this article regarding "lovesickness," was to discover if mental illness and love were linked in a way that would cause one to display hysterical or bizarre behaviors. Since psychology is the study of human behavior, research gives the impression that favors that the love and mental illness connection not be excluded. And since the soul is the realm of the mind, will and emotions, indeed this mania type of love will cause the soul to yearn and even experience a wounding. Again, let it be emphasized that the reason for the sorrow is caused by the type of love in the area of the soul realm of man's make-up.

This selfish mania form of love may certainly become dangerous. Resentments of anger and bitterness arise and it is most difficult when one in a relationship is left alone for another. This is when it really becomes outrageous and most apparent; the strong emotions manifest when relationships sever because someone else has invaded and violated boundaries. As one partner adamantly attempts to work on the relationship, this one is now blamed for stalking. It now becomes a crazy form of love with yelling, fighting, and storming off in furious outbursts. This form of love in a relationship is what sociology calls "mania love" and is unquestionably rather nauseating. Its characteristics are jealousy, possessiveness, obsessiveness, and strong dependence. This "mania" love literally causes sickness in those who possess this crazy type of love. It has been known to cause headaches, anxiety, sleeplessness, depression, intestinal disorders and even suicide. In this poor sick *soul* of man, which is his mind, the nature of thoughts which grip him in strongholds are the imaginations of being rejected or that his lover will desire another. The thoughts have him bound to believing that his much-loved will do him wrong with betrayal; hence the needs to be shown ample amounts of love and attention by his partner are necessary for his own sustenance. If not given what he thrives on, he becomes a mad-man or "maniac" by displaying fits of rage.

Given these points, the soul of man has a necessity for love. For most, it is a love that differs from any other; it is one's own perception of how they should be loved. If not given what is needed for their subsistence, they become malnourished and eventually diseased with an addiction to be loved. Like the baby born with a cocaine habit craving a fix, so the soul of man too craves for his own sort of "fix" of gratification and perceives this is his answer for survival.

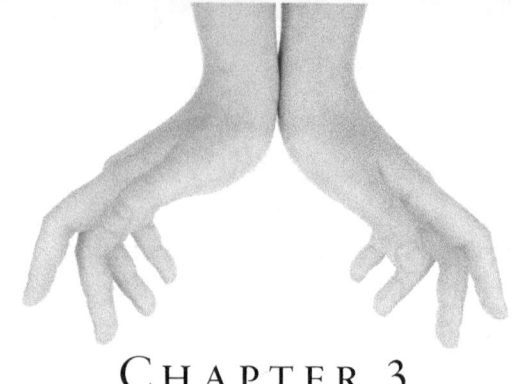

CHAPTER 3

Addiction to Loving Self

The Compulsive Cycles of Love Addicts

The "love" that has been described thus far is nowhere near the "True Love Remedy" that the Apostle Paul conveys to the Corinthians. He gives a description of this divine love—never failing and always enduring; it is love that is not arrogant or conceited with pride. All other types of love have given proof of expression only under certain of man's preferred condition, consequently causing much grief. Man's soulish desire is a self-seeking form of love to boost his ego with satisfaction and pleasure; it shows forth 99% of the time in their preference to receive rather than to give. Because man's soul has become addicted to himself, what takes priority is choosing "the god of self" in order to get what he wants over letting others get what they want. When one has an addiction to loving self, he too most likely has an addiction to love. He NEEDS to be shown love and the need then becomes triggered. He lives in a fantasy world looking for someone who is attractive and having it all together. He expects any person he involves himself with to play out his imaginary life with him to mollify his habituated high. Pia Mellody, in her book, Facing Love Addiction, (New York, NY: HarperCollins Publisher, 1992), pp.22-23, gives the characteristics of *Love Addicts*. She writes:

> "Classic Love Addicts move through a cycle of emotional states as they meet someone, try to live out the childhood fantasy of being rescued, live in denial about the inappropriate

behavior of their partner, experience frustration and failure because it seems that nothing they do will make it work, try harder, come out of denial about the inappropriate behavior of the partner, begin obsessing and behaving compulsively, then begin all over again to fantasize about the relationship. Each time they cycle through this pattern, the experience becomes more and more toxic to the Love Addict. The Love Addict is attracted to the seduction and apparent "Power" of the Love Avoidant. Love Addicts meet someone attractive to them, usually a person who is very involved in a lot of things and seems to be managing them very well. This person's apparent power is attractive to Love Addicts because, as we have seen, Love Addicts have been set up to believe they are unable to take care of themselves and are looking for someone who can do the job. Also, if the person is a Love Avoidant he will be behind a wall of seduction, which makes the Love Addict feel special. The Love Addict's need to feel loved then gets triggered.

Often people who are attracted into addictive relationships talk about "love at first sight." I believe we should be cautious when we are experiencing love at first sight; it may really be "addiction at first sight."

The God of Self

By all means, this kind of love is surely not the medicine for the "yearning soul" seeking a redeemer to remedy his disorder. Rather, it is a love poison that enters the veins of the soul to suck out the life of man. This "adoration" is not even reality; it is entirely fantasy which brings lustful pleasure for only a season, then becomes so warped that it inaugurates the destruction of the soul. Little by little, like a flesh-eating bacterium, man's life is withering away, though he may not even realize it. The destroyer will eventually eat away every part of him and deliver him to his grave. The central problem to the one who is addicted to loving self is PRIDE; it is the very diagnosis given to the first spiritual being exiled from the heavenly courts of the Almighty. The "the pride of life" is the ultimate sin of one who becomes enthroned with loving self rather than God. He has made himself the "god" of himself and worships himself alone. Kyle Idleman, author of the book, <u>Gods at War: Defeating the Idols That Battle for Your Heart</u>, (Grand Rapids, Michigan: Zondervan, 2013) pp. 229-230, gives the symptoms of those who have created a god within themselves. He writes:

> "One symptom is arrogance. I'm always right. My way is the best way. The god of me won't listen to the wisdom of others...
>
> So let me ask you this. When was the last time you made one of the following statements: 'I was wrong'; 'You were right'; 'I should have listened to you'; 'I like your idea better'? Even when we don't realize it, a touch of arrogance may be present.
>
> Another symptom that surfaces when I start to worship the god of me is insecurity. The god of me is consumed with what others think and terrified of trying something and failing. You can't help but be self-conscious, because when you're god, it's all about you.
>
> How about defensiveness? Have you ever found yourself taking the slightest suggestion, the blandest criticism, as a personal attack? What makes people this way? Well, when you're god, you must be perfect, and no one else could possibly be in a position to criticize you.
>
> The god of me will make you lonely, because you can't handle equals. You certainly can't handle authority. You need people who constantly reaffirm that it's all about you.
>
> Listen to what God says: 'In the pride of your heart you say, 'I am a god; I sit on the throne of a god'...But you are a mere mortal and not a god, though you think you are as wise as a god' (Ezek. 28:2). The god of me is the most relentless idol of them all."

Mr. Idleman further states that this type of god loving self will not satisfy. It is the type of love that is short lived, and at risk for infidelity; the lack of emotional warmth displays dishonesty and violent behaviors. It is the twisted love that fails time and time again still leaving the soul of man destitute in the process causing pain to another. It is a decision that one makes that will never bring tranquility if the mind of man is not dealt with. If he is not shown or given the truth of unending love and true peace, man continues to live in chaos.

When this god of self, arrives at a place where he decides to opt out because he no longer feels worshiped by his "significant other," his sick ego of dissatisfaction arrives at a conclusion that there is no reason he should waste his time in trying to explain his abandoning cold-hearted actions. By this time his all-inclusive soul man[14] has become king of his own domain. He breaks the news to the very person he avows to love, to the one he has shared his deepest sentiments and dreams with, all because he is a lover of his own soul. He tells her of his identifiable discovery within himself, that the person who has shared his bed for many years, only in body but not in soul, is no longer the significant other after all.

After the honeymoon and duration of seasons, the feelings towards his wife disintegrate, and although he shares the same bed, he finds himself in deep thought wishing, dreaming or fantasizing about another. Moreover, he now becomes the absent husband while his hot meals turn cold three or four times a week. Night after night, his wife in black silk waits for his return, hoping to catch the flicker in his eyes once again towards her. She continues to ask herself, while saturating her pillow with hurtful tears, "Where have I gone wrong in this marriage?" While the husband is caught up in his own sick world of love triangles, his sickness permeates to his children who wonder where daddy has gone.

The question arises, "How can two beautiful people with beautiful children, and with a beautiful home, fall out of love so easily from one day to the next, and then attach with another so quickly?" This sick soul tie with another destroys the lives of those around him, and yet he fails to realize what one bad move can cause. It is as a small cigarette butt that is thrown out of a window without having given it thought for a moment that this miniscule grass fire would turn into a forest fire,

---

[14] When referring to the "soul of man," or "man," note the writer refers to both women and men. The cause of break-ups or broken marriages, have been caused by both men and women who are selfish and self-seeking to bring pleasure to their own souls—comprised of the mind, will and emotions. The love sick soul operates in his own will not thinking of the extreme consequences of his actions.

destroying the lives of so many innocent people. The effects are the wounds of infirmed hearts that have been shattered into pieces; now, the anguish of pain transforms into scars that must be dealt with for the rest of their entire lives. If this is the type of love that is the answer to the lost soul of man, something is definitely wrong.

The writer of 2 Timothy 3:1-6, gives the exact description of how the world is today in these perilous times. He states, *"This know also, that in the last days perilous times shall come. For men shall be **lovers of their own selves**, covetous, boasters, proud, blasphemers, disobedient to parents, unthankful, unholy, Without natural affection, trucebreakers, false accusers, incontinent, fierce, despisers of those that are good, Traitors, heady, highminded, lovers of pleasures more than lovers of God; Having a form of godliness, but denying the power thereof: from such turn away. For of this sort are they which creep into houses, and lead captive silly women laden with sins, led away with divers lusts,"* (KJV).

The Love Hazardous to Kill

It's no marvel that the world is filled with what psychiatrists' call "emotional disorders." Yes, indeed the souls of men are in a disorderly array, but these educated doctors cannot cure what ails the inner part of man with a pill or a motivational speech that accomplishes nothing. Until the despondent soul arrives at a detour or a roadblock of life and takes heed to the warning signs boldly stating, "Wrong Way" and "Hazardous—Do Not Enter," he will never arrive at a destination of true contentment. The bewildered soul must reach to close his own self-seeking path, drawing nigh to a realization that the need is greater than what he has ever imagined. His egotistical GPS of pleasing self has gotten him befuddled, and the path he has taken his entire life thus far, has transported him to a wrong destination called, "NOWHERE." The many different pathways he has continued to select throughout life may only pacify for a season, but not for an eternity.

Throughout his pursuit of that which he is not sure of himself, a Watchman appears at different times to show him the right way, but he refuses to listen to any other messages besides his own. As he searches diligently for what he believes may calm his restlessness, he continues to consider this Watchman; occasionally he will request help from him to assist in finding what he longs for. Just as the Watchman is about to share more details about his journey, diversion soars into his soul as he witnesses a pleasant looking route. This itinerary leads him to a very attractive slender 5'9 brunette with contours that would make a Van Gogh painting melt from the heat she sparks. Her red hot lips and long flattery eyelashes grab the attention of not only him, but other malefactors gazing upon her like wolves ready to attack. He then jolts away from this watchman and soars like a bat out of hell towards "red delicious" to now gain her attention. As he furthers himself away from the watchman, he can only hear the distant and muffled yelling, "YOUR WIFE AWAITS YOU AND YOUR CHILDREN NEED YOU RIGHT NOW...COME BACK... I SAY, COME BACK!" He almost turns back, but refuses to listen to the still small voice within himself. The lust of his eyes and the lust of his flesh overshadow the redeemable and comforting words that finally could bring him the salvation he needs. It is now a battle competing with himself to gain the attention of this devil in disguise. Little does he know he will not have to work hard at all; for she is the woman in sleek veneer who is planted with purpose; she is the very one who keeps him, and others, from the abundant life his watchman intends for him to experience.

Her being used by Satan has been not only for the men of this world, but also to create hostility and anguish for the wives who hate her with a passion to kill. The watchman can only see him from afar and hopes for his return with right intentions. Saddened by his refusal to return, he then whispers in that still small voice while interceding, "I pray for your return my son, for you are blinded to your own lust of pleasure; you are addicted to foolish stupid love that is conditional and looking for love in all the wrong places, you have been persuaded, yet again have been warned." The writer of Proverbs conveys this aspect as he too tries to persuade a young lad to hearken to the words of the truth. He states: *"My son, keep thy father's commandment, and forsake not the law of thy mother: Bind them continually upon thine heart, and tie them about thy neck. When thou goest, it shall lead thee; when thou sleepest, it shall keep thee; and when thou awakest, it shall talk with thee. For the commandment is a lamp; and the law is light; and reproofs of instruction are the way of life: To keep thee from the evil woman, from the flattery of the tongue of a strange woman. Lust not after her beauty in thine heart; neither let her take thee with her eyelids. For by means of a whorish woman a man is brought to a piece of bread: and the adultress will hunt for the precious life. Can a man take fire in his bosom, and his clothes not be burned? Can one go upon hot coals, and his feet not be burned? So he that goeth in to his neighbour's wife; whosoever toucheth her shall not be innocent. Men do not despise a thief, if he steal to satisfy his soul when he is hungry; But if he be found, he shall restore sevenfold; he shall give all the substance of his house. But* **whoso committeth adultery with a woman lacketh understanding: he that doeth it destroyeth his own soul.** *A wound and dishonour shall he get; and his reproach shall not be wiped away. For jealousy is the rage of a man: therefore he will not spare in the day of vengeance. He will not regard any ransom; neither will he rest content, though thou givest many gifts"* (Proverbs 6:20-35, KJV).

Refusal of the Watchman's Voice

Unquestionably, the god of self-love is nowhere near the brand of affection that elixirs the longing soul of man. This powerful four-letter word called "LOVE" which man connects to "self" contaminates the true meaning of what love is to portray. This self-love is a destroyer of the soul and will permeate the rest of his entire being if not dealt with. Man's own way is not the response that man seeks to fulfill his longing lust for true love. This love he searches for springs up throughout his life, more frequently as he gets older. This Watchman earnestly tries to draw his attention, to direct him towards this *Genuine Love* he yearns for. Man's refusal to walk in any other way besides his own, even he does not comprehend, causes the deterioration of his insides. The Prophet Jeremiah states that when one has made an idol of self and is full of pride, the destruction and dwindling of man is soon to follow. He declares: *"Your [object of] horror (your idol) has deceived you, and the pride of your heart [has deceived you], O you who dwell in the clefts of the rock [Sela or Petra], who hold and occupy the height of the hill. Though you make your nest as high as the eagle's, I will bring you down from there, says the Lord"* (Jeremiah 49:16, AMP).

Although he is warned on several occasions to take the path of the Watchman, he once again fuels his own egocentric self from the prideful depths of his own soul to rule his life. He allows once again for the devil to come in and operate in the very place he is so familiar with; it is a place of dark proud souls, full of egotism and raising hell in arrogance.

This kind of love is hard core and maneuvers in manipulation to get what one wants. It is a vile inhumane and unsympathetic love that causes ordinary and stable folks to become fuming madmen with the potential to kill the very one they claim to love. One wonders where this sick soul acquires his learning, and whether Casanova instilled in him the infectious virus of insensitivity. Yes, indeed man has become addicted to loving himself.

CHAPTER 4

"Hide-And-Go-Seek, Daddy?"

Apparently, little boys are not being taught to be gentlemen any longer, and little girls are not trained to value themselves highly. Times have undeniably altered the way of thinking for manhood and womanhood. The days of family togetherness are long gone, the days that portrayed the iconic and ideal suburban families of the mid-twentieth century, "Father Knows Best" and "Leave it to Beaver." What once was looked upon as the flawless family has now been turned into a joke by so many. The father, who once was the role model to his sons, who desired to be like him, and who was the example to his daughters of the kind of man they should look for, has vanished. The many children of the world today wonder and will ask the same question, "Who will teach me to be the kind of man I should be, and how shall I treat a woman; and what kind of woman shall I marry?" Or, "Who will teach me to be the kind of woman I should be; who will teach me what type of man I should marry someday; and who will teach me about peer pressure and about the boys who are already acting weird towards me; and who will teach me how to love?"

Innocent Love Turns Erotic

Now the responsibility of educating the children after school hours has been left to the internet and television programs. HBO, Showtime, Teen-Nick, MTV, just to name a few, are the channels where information is taken from and stored away in the minds of the next generations. And, when these children are left alone to fend for themselves, they learn what

Hollywood portrays love to be. They grow up believing that nothing is wrong by acquiring multiple lovers, cohabitating instead of getting married, having extra marital affairs and having sex before marriage. They too become curious about the opposite sex, and nowadays, even relations with the same sex. Internet, television and other peers have taught innocent little children to become erotic by the time they arrive at middle school age. They too search for answers wanting to find the truth of "LOVE," the weird and mysterious feelings they are now experiencing towards the ones they sit near to in the cafeteria lunch room. They ask. "Is this that I am feeling, the feeling of love?" When parents are not around to teach their children the right way, they will most definitely get their teaching elsewhere. And when this occurs, they are in for massive obstacles, ones that have been created by the parents, and mainly by the absent father.

The Absent Father Syndrome

When the hard-working and loving father who used to make family his priority is no longer present, but chooses to remain absent from the picture, chaos is inevitable. Instead, the house is totally empty with no sound of mother to greet her children because now she must work two jobs trying to provide for her family. Homework assistance from father and mother has become a thing of the past; playing catch with sons is not even thought about in this day and age. Because she took on another shift to make ends meet, by the time mother arrives, she is too tired to open any school book with her child to go over assignments. In addition, the missing father hopes he receives no call from his ex-wife asking to help with more child support. And, do not even think about asking, "Hide-And-Go-Seek, Daddy?" Daddy is nowhere to be found; he is lost with another woman, cohabitating so he can be sure of not being responsible for yet another support bill. This poor child does not have the privilege of asking such a question—the father is simply not there to raise his own. Because the father has chosen to be absent from the lives of his children, and refuses to make time to play hide-and-go-seek, these same children grow up playing their own version of "Hide-And-Go-Seek." They now look for love in all the wrong places and find themselves in a huge disarray of love trilogies themselves.

The Misfit Generation Seek Love Too

The absent father, lacking integrity, proves to cause a generation of misfits who learn about sex through the internet and obtain their knowledge on how to treat their "hoochie—mamas" from the monthly issue of Hustler magazine. By the same token, these once sweet, innocent little girls, who were to be women of virtue, surprisingly wind up on the home page of "Girls Gone Wild-Spring Break 2014." Most assuredly they are learning, but it is not the knowledge of truth, the truth that will keep them from the darkness of this adulterous generation. The writer of 2 Timothy 3:7 continues to state, *"...ever learning, and never able to come to the knowledge of the truth"* (KJV). This generation is in for a rude awakening for they are being destroyed for lack of TRUE KNOWLEDGE that is able to save their souls.

The Wounds of Shattered Arrows

Where there is no knowledge of love springing forth from accountable parents who take the time to train their children in the right ways, terror is born. This seed that has been planted grows into weeds of trepidation. Because these children grow up to be fearful and have no real security in their lives, the future of so many has been destroyed. They should have been able to go somewhere in life, they should have had the opportunity to move forward and shoot like an arrow to great heights. Instead, before they can even be launched out, these "arrows" become broken and unable to be used. Before even thinking they can be utilized, these arrows need fixing. Psalms 127:3-5 states, *"Lo, children are an heritage of the Lord: and the fruit of the womb is His reward. As **arrows** are in the hand of a mighty man; so are children of the youth. Happy is the man that hath his quiver full of them: they shall not be ashamed, but they shall speak with the enemies in the gate"* (KJV). The fathers that were to be mighty men, holding in their hand the arrows representing their children, are now MIA. He has chosen to go AWOL, and the circumstances that have risen in the lives of their children have shattered and have hindered any kind of movement.

Though it may seem that the writer chooses to put at fault the father, or the man, in this whole ordeal, yet it is true. The father has been ordained by God to be the leader of his wife and children. He is to be the pastor of his home who guides and direct his family in the right way leading to the truth. Although the exhortation and reproof is for both father and mother, it is emphasized towards the man who should have been the "man of the house," displaying love and safety. The wife and children ought to have been given the beautiful gift of experiencing family warmth, a refuge of love and shelter for protection. The father should have been the authorative figure in the family, raising little boys to become men of integrity, hard workers, providers and loving husbands to their wives. He was to be a shield for these innocent little girls and boys who have been violated by the baby sitter, family friend, or even himself; he was to have been looked upon and trusted to provide security, instead of fear and insecurity.

Because of this inattentive father and the lack of true love, the horrific nightmares of the past inhabit the souls of these disrupted lives. These little lambs were to grow strong and mighty. Now, the encroaching thoughts at night bring about restless hours of sleep as she requests God for "that man" not to enter her room for one more dreadful throbbing of anguish, all because the absent father refuses to be responsible and to show love towards his family. There is no father present to ask, "Hide-And-Go-Seek, Daddy?" Pastor T. D. Jakes, author of the book, Woman Thou art Loosed: Healing the Wounds of the Past, (Shippensburg, PA: Treasure House, 1993), pp. 19-20, states that it is for the arrows of this generation that we must pray. He writes:

> "It is for the arrows of this generation that we must pray—
> they who are being aimed at the streets and drugs and
> perversion. Not all of them, but some of them have been
> broken in the quiver! I write to every empty-eyed child I
> have ever seen sit at my desk with tears and trembling lips
> struggling to tell the unmentionable secret. I write to the
> trembling voice of every caller who spoke into a telephone
> a secret they could not keep and could not tell. I write to
> every husband who holds a woman every night, a child lost
> in space, a rosebud crushed before you met her, a broken
> arrow shaking in the quiver. I write to every lady who hides
> behind silk dresses and leather purses a terrible secret that
> makeup can't seem to cover and long showers will not

wash. Some people call them abused children. Some call them victimized. Some call them statistics. But I call them broken arrows.

Whose hand is this that fondles the bare, flat chest of a little girl? Whose fingers linger upon the flesh he helped to create? Why has the love that should be mama's come to snuggle under daughter? 'Someone tell me how to rinse the feeling of fingers off my mind?" This is the cry of little children all over the country. This is the cry of worried minds clutching dolls, riding bicycles—little girls and even little boys sitting on school buses who got more for Christmas than they could ever show and tell. The Church must realize that the adult problems we are fighting to correct are often rooted in the ashes of childhood experiences."

Man's refusal to step into that precise place of fatherhood has caused many sons to either become homosexuals or very feminine males emulating the female baby sitter who spent hours with him while the single mother worked her two jobs. Thus, the decisions of the absent father to move to another city because of his hatred toward his ex-wife, and to hardly visit his son have caused his son to seek after lovers of his own gender. In addition, the father has the audacity to resent his son for his own (the father's) refusal to be the father he should have been all along. The need for true love is, without a doubt, essential, but the simple fact is that man looks for love in all the wrong places because he has not been taught and trained in the proper way.

In the same manner, little girls seek the wrong kind of man because they have no example of a real man to teach them how they should be treated. Instead, they settle for a low-life immature boy trapped in the body of a 35-year old who still spends his time playing video games instead of seeking a real job or career to provide for his unborn child who is due any day. She finally gets the strength to leave the slothful man in her life but soon finds herself in an even deeper situation than before. She finally assumes she meets the man of her dreams, handsome and at first, very charming, who promises to give her the world. He also promises he will eventually leave his wife of 15 years because he wants to live happily ever after with her. So she has been wrongly convinced as she patiently waits for her lover's promise to come true. She anticipates a pleasurable life, but when the months turn into years, she now has two illegitimate children out of wedlock, or, what the neighbors call, "bastards." She cries while her children, happy as could be, wonder why mommy is so sad. She cries for her children who have no name to possess; no father to spend time with, and no role model of a father's love.

The father of her children, only known as uncle Javan, whose name ironically means "deceiver" and to "make sad," still visits her occasionally, but not often. With the same old promise to keep her bound to him, she long-sufferingly stands by while reading the announcement in the daily newspaper of her lover's wife delivering twin sons that will proudly carry his name forever. She begins to ponder on her own children's inheritance and wonders if her children will attain a part of their birthright. Little does she know that neither her name nor the names of her two children are to be found in any legal documents; the money given to her to aid with the children's support was all given in cash. She never got around to reporting to the state and declaring the valid evidence of the father's name because she was deceivably swayed by her pronounced romantic lover, the well-known Mr. Javan B. Hermon, owner of the most optimal business in town.

In his own thoughts, he is safe and secure because she is not the first to claim his fatherhood of her unlawful children; this mother is just another money-hungry, desperate woman who seeks to gain a buck. When she becomes angry enough, she will get the courage to finally tell his wife the truth that has been hidden for many years. As she hears the tender voice of her lover's wife on the other end of the phone say, "Hello, may I help you?" she whispers back the word "Hello." As soon as the wife hears this other voice's response, she yells towards her husband, "Oh, it's just another one of your money hungry whores; you best tell them to stop calling me!!" She then hears the loud clashing sound of a hung up phone against her ear. Now, the shattered pieces of her heart are in need of repair. She hurts so badly, and does not know what she will do or where she will go. She lives her life continually in fear, not having that sense of security and love she longs for. She asks the question, "Where did I go wrong in all of this?" Though she believes this turmoil she is experiencing is her fault and her failure, she is not altogether right. Her pain actually began when her own father made that most irresponsible and thoughtless judgment—to be absent from his wife and children.

The only cure now for that beaten and battered soul is what the writer of I John 4:18 declares to overpower the fear and terror one is facing. He states, *"There is no fear in love; but perfect love casteth out fear: because fear hath torment. He that feareth is not made perfect in love"* (KJV). Where is this "perfect love" to be found to quiet her bitter soul that wishes to die at that very moment? The pain to her is so unbearable; she feels as if she is going crazy. She is all alone with her precious children who wonder why mommy cries so much. Just like mommy needs an elixir for her soul, that remedy of healing, her children will soon desire that same love, peace and security from another.

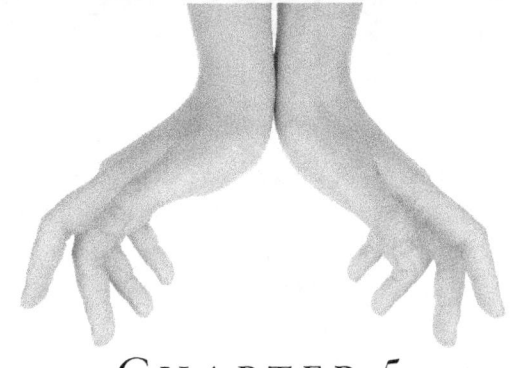

CHAPTER 5

Love in Religion: Which God, Which Love?

When discussing a solution for man's crushed soul, many believe that religion is the answer and perhaps a ceremonial cleansing will do the job. The agonizing despairing soul that aches and cries out for rescue turns to spiritualism with the hope of finding a key to unravel his chains of darkness and coming to a place of enlightened tranquility. The journey proceeds on a road of tears towards a variety of gods, hoping and praying for that elixir that will cure the infirm ailment of numbness. These endeavors are en route towards religions such as Hinduism, Buddhism, Islam, and Christianity, with an anticipation to discover genuine peace and pleasure for the broken heart. Could the healing agent possibly be found in a ritual, a ceremonial chant or an incantation for coveted peace?

What must first be inquired is, which religion or which god will give what is needed to deliver him from the wretched feeling of deep pain. Salvation that conveys love, peace and security are the essentials the dire soul searches. Just as there are many man-made remedies for the hurting soul of man, likewise there are way too many gods and different kinds of love. Because of this, the world is full of confusion, running to and fro seeking for that right one—the one that will deliver true contentment. Man seeks a redeemer, and if not found, there remains the lack of fulfillment in the essence of mankind until the influx of the soul unites with the "God of Power that comprises preservation," and thus instigates a pursuit for love's elixir.

The analysis of the different types of religious doctrines and gods will perhaps give insight as to which is the truth that leads to the true love and peace for which man seeks. In this quest, there is an anticipation of receiving wisdom and knowledge on how to give and accept love, for one cannot properly give love until they first know how to accept love; and one cannot know love, until they know the true pathway that leads to true love. In addition, before handling any form of "LOVE," one must come to realize that love is not "just love." There are many different types of love and therefore it is confusing to the soul of man, who roams in darkness blinded and kept from the truth. An assessment for the purpose of discovering if perhaps any of these gods will offer salvation originated by love, will perhaps shed some light conveying illumination. So, the intrusive question still remains to the confounded thinker who continues to ask, "Which God," and "Which Love?" What truth will calm the soul of unrest and deliver comfort and peace to the forsaken mind who inquires far and wide for revelation. Or, will it be discovered that there are numerous conflicts among these religions and their gods which endeavor to offer liberation to no avail?

The Hindu Religion

The Hindu religion will first be looked at and discussed to recognize their creed and to search for a god of salvation and an awareness of a genuine love. Hendrik M. Vroom, author of <u>Religions and the Truth</u>, (Grand Rapids, Michigan: William B. Eerdmans Publishing Company, 1989), p. 105, attempts to draw honest conclusions regarding the religion of Hinduism and their god; he gathers interpretations from those who are committed followers within these customs and traditions. Mr. Vroom states that the gods in the Hindu religion can sometimes be fascinating and sometimes terrifying in reality. He says that gods are not constantly good and the devils are not constantly bad, which is reflected by the myths about the origin of suffering and misfortune. He writes:

> "Traces of the original indigenous religion are plain in the later phases of the history of Hinduism. In the course of time, large shifts occur in the world of the gods. Some gods lose significance while others move into the foreground, until at last the 'Hindu trinity' emerges: Brahma, Visnu,

and Siva, of whom the latter two are especially revered. Numerous elements from the old folk religion were preserved in the popular religion, according to many commentators. People point out the worship of Siva's linga, a practice still widespread in modern India; it is a phallic symbol which, in combination with the female symbol, is seen as an expression of the encompassing unity of all things. 'Thus,' writes Diana Eck, 'it is *the* symbol of the unity of the Hindu Universe' (Eck, Banaras, p.105; cf. Chaudhuri, p. 229.) In later mythology, numerous elements from the earlier indigenous religion can be discovered."

Vroom shares a glimpse into one of the well-known myths or "narrative cycles" to further recognize the concepts of their belief. He continues:

"One of the best known narrative cycles is about Krisna, one of the *avataras* (earthly form of appearance) of Visnu among mankind. Krisna was born in a miraculous fashion and was saved from the hand of the enemy. He grew up among shepherds, and, not to be overlooked, shepherdesses. His many remarkable deeds were but so many notches on his belt for the young hero. The most familiar narratives, however, concern his encounters with *gopis*, the wives of the shepherds. He entices them out of their homes with his admirably beautiful flute playing. Roused by longing for Krisna they abandon mop, brood, husband, and honour. He dances with them. He steals their clothes while they are taking a sacred bath in the river. He leaves them in the lurch. The love scenes with one of the *gopis*, Radha, are elaborately described and have been narrated and depicted countless times. Their unification is more than romantic love or fornication. For Krisna is in reality the Most High. That is how the myth relates it as well: Madhusudana (that is, Krisna), whose nature is immeasurable, appeared as a young man in this fashion and played with the shepherds' wives, day and night. He whose real form is as pervasive as the wind lives as the Lord in these women, and in their spouses, as in all creatures. Just as ether, fire, earth, water, and wind are in all creatures, so the Lord Himself, who permeates the universe, abides in all things.

Radha is Krisna; God is in everyone. According to some currents, the love of Radha and Krisna symbolizes the unity of all worldly plurality in God. It simultaneously points up the longing of the human soul to experience spiritual union with God... The realization of the ultimate union of all things with God is vitalized by the myths, stories, statues, and portraits of folk religion" Ibid., 111-112.

Mr. Vroom was definitely on target when he stated that the gods of Hindu can sometimes be fascinating and terrifying in reality. Particularly odd, is the account, or myth, of Krisna, who has encounters with the wives of the shepherds, how he lures them with his tempting flute playing. Radha/Krisna, is intensely dissimilar to the true and living God written about in the Holy Bible, Who in no way is a tempter of any. There is no need for any kind of enticing sound who would lure people to Him. Yes, He desires for all to come to the knowledge of His Truth but no need to use such devices to draw people to Himself. The Bible declares, *"Let no man say when he is tempted, I am tempted of God: for God cannot be tempted with evil, neither tempteth he any man:"* (James 1:13, KJV).

The Religion of Buddhism

When I think of the religion of Buddhism, I cannot help to be reminded of Angela Basset portraying the role of Tina Turner in the movie, "What's Love Got to Do with It?" This was the path which Tina Turner ventured towards to bring her a sense of tranquility in the midst of heart-ache. While being beaten and battered, in every kind of way, by the hands of her abusive husband, Ike Turner, she sought for a place of peace. Through the practices of Buddhism, which embrace deep truths concerning life's suffering and the striving for enlightenment, Tina Turner pushed herself through life's anguish. These practices incorporated doctrines such as the Eightfold Path and the Four Noble Truths, along with everyday chants with meditations. Thus, we shall cross the threshold into the religion of Buddhism to seek their truth and perceptions regarding their creed.

The religion of Buddhism was founded by Siddhartha Gautama, who is also known as "Buddha," which means the "Enlightened One." Buddha followers are known to practice meditation; they also incorporate specific doctrines of Buddha in order to reach a place of enlightenment, or wellbeing. In having a deep understanding of life's essence and suffering, the goal is striving for contentment. Central findings are of "The Four Noble Truths" which are teachings of four summarized doctrines by Buddhists. They all deal with the truth of suffering, its origin, the cessation and the path which leads to the cessation of suffering and thus leading to the paths of salvation. Chaya Rao, author of Buddhist, (Middletown, DE: LCPublifish LLC, 2014), pp. 9-11, shares on the principals of the Buddhist creed concerning these noble truths. Rao affirms that if there is one characteristic of Buddhism that defines the unabridged belief, it is these following truths. Rao states:

"The truth of suffering (dukkha)

The word dukkha represents anything that is conditional, anything that passes or is not permanent. The exact translation of the first Noble Truth is 'life is suffering.' This may seem a little odd at first, especially if you are new to Buddhism. However, Buddha went on to explain what this truth is all about. The idea behind it is to understand the fact that we are not immortal, nor are any of our feelings, or suffering. Everything that starts and has an end is dukkha, be it happiness, sadness, grief, or anything else for that matter. Buddha stressed that we must understand 'self' before we consider the concepts of life and death.

The truth of the cause of suffering (samudaya)

The second truth is the reason we suffer, and that is because we crave what we do not have. This is a universal truth – our wants are unlimited. As soon as we have something, we want more. We look toward other people's plates and we tend to envy. We wish to acquire what we do not have, while disregarding what we do have. This is jealousy, and there are few things worse than jealousy.

Buddha taught that by going after such worldly things, we lose ourselves and our path. From material things to opinions, ideas, and whatnot, we get so involved in ourselves that when things do not go as we wish them to, we grieve. That, Buddha stresses, is what leads to suffering...

...By eliminating this preoccupation, we can relieve ourselves and gain true bliss.

The truth of the end of suffering (nirhodha)

Having explained what suffering is and what causes it, Buddha then taught how to cure it. The cure, he said, could be found through practice. By making ourselves stronger, and not giving in to our never-ending wants, we can reach the stage of enlightenment that will help us reach a state of Nirvana.

The idea is to keep on trying, to keep looking the other way and controlling ourselves when we are faced with our overwhelming desires. It may be the hardest thing we ever have to do, but it is the route to real liberation.

The truth of the path that frees us from suffering (magga)

By stressing over and over again on the concept that believing is not enough, Buddha taught that his teaching need be molded into a lifestyle. It is not enough to know and speak. You must exercise it."

The Islam Religion

According to the Islamic tradition, observance of religious obligations and rituals are strictly required by God, who they call Allah, and whose prophet is Mohammed. In a revelation delivered to this prophet, Mohammed, by the angel Gabriel, Allah makes himself known as the "Merciful and the Compassionate." His sacredness and soundness have the supreme preeminence and is known to be compassionate by making himself known to people by delivering life's guiding principles. He pardons people of much and assigns positions to those who please him; he will likewise judge on the last day, distributing rewards for good deeds done and punishing those who committed the bad.

Luke H. Hardy, author of <u>Islam Religion</u>, (Lexington, KY: Independently Published, 2016), pp. 24-26, shares on the basic fundamentals of the Islamic belief. Mr. Hardy states that there are basic beliefs of Islam and if one is to be a true Muslim, then he/she must believe in all. He writes:

> **There is only one god and he is singular and incomparable.** You must call upon no other. You must pray to no other. To say that we have been created out of his image and likeness would be to besmirch his name.
>
> **Angels exist and are to be honored.** Angels worship and obey Allah. They act out his will.
>
> **Allah provided his messengers with revelations through his books.** The purpose of the Quran is to provide guidance for mankind. God's word in the Quran must be protected from any kind of corruption or alteration which will lead to its misinterpretation.
>
> **God has prophets.** Some of these prophets include Adam, Abraham, Moses, Noah, and Jesus. They all serve as his messengers and yet none of them possess the divine qualities of God. However, Allah's last message was revealed to no other than Muhammad. To put it plainly, Muhammad is considered as the last prophet.
>
> **In the Day of Judgment, everyone will be resurrected so that they may be judged by Allah.** All will be judged according to what they believed in and what they had done. A person who dies believing in gods other than Allah and following the teaching of prophets other than Muhammad, will lose his place in Paradise. Simply put, you have to be Muslim in order to be accepted in heaven...
>
> Allah records everything that transpires and that which will transpire. Simply put, he knows what decision you will make even before you make it. He knows whether you will end up in heaven or in hell even before you pass on to the afterlife."

These beliefs of Islam are quite interesting in comparison to other religions; it is difficult to comprehend how Allah would already know everyone's destination. Here on earth, every man has their own free will to make choices, and it is these choices that leads to one's own destination. Yes, the true and living God of Christianity does know all things but this is why Jesus is at the right hand of the Father, making intercession for His people. Jesus prays that His people would make the right choices in this life and that they would remain on the right path that leads to eternal life, not destruction. The writer of Romans declares, *"Who is he that condemneth? It is Christ that died, yea rather, that is risen again, **who is even at the right hand of God, who also maketh intercession for us.**"* (Romans 8:34, KJV).

To add, the Bible declares that Jesus sent His Holy Spirit as the Helper to help His people make the right decisions; He would likewise guide them to His Truth, which is the Word of God. To those who have not yet received the free gift of salvation through Jesus, are not left out in no way according to God's Word; on the contrary, all are given the same opportunity to accept Jesus into their lives and to live for Him. However, not all will choose to accept Him as their personal Savior due to their God-given free will, in spite of the Holy Spirit convicting them of their sins. This sounds more of a loving, compassionate and merciful God—One Who would deal with people, even in their lost and dire state. Of course, God desires that all would receive Him and this is why the Spirit of God is always working to save the lost and dying world. His will is that not one soul would perish and be condemned to hell. God's Word declares, *"7 But I tell you the truth, it is to your advantage that I go away; for if I do not go away, the Helper (Comforter, Advocate, Intercessor—Counselor, Strengthener, Standby) will not come to you; but if I go, I will send Him (the Holy Spirit) to you [to be in close fellowship with you].8 And He, when He comes, **will convict the world about [the guilt of] sin [and the need for a Savior]**, and about righteousness, and about judgment: 9 about sin [and the true nature of it], because they do not believe in Me [and My message]; 10 about righteousness [personal integrity and godly character],…"* (John 16:7-10, AMP).

Christianity: Religion or Relationship?

For the most part, there proves numerous conflicts among these religions and their gods which endeavor to offer liberation to no avail. Now, the attempts to discern into the religion of Christianity will hopefully assist in finding the concrete evidence so many seek to deliver clarity. According to the Holy Bible, Christianity is not a religion and likewise there are no other gods, religions or manmade doctrines that can compare to the **God of Love.** His Love manifests no limits or boundaries pertaining to mankind; His love operates not in the traditions or rituals of man, but it is through a loving, gracious and merciful relationship with His beloved creation. God's Love is so great that He offers salvation; it is a free gift given by the Heavenly Father that requires no work of any merit in order to acquire His redemption. Ephesians 2:8-9 declares, *"For by grace are ye saved through faith; and that not of yourselves: it is the gift of God: Not of works, lest any man should boast"* (KJV).

He is not like Brahman,[15] the god of the Hindu religion, who implores that all mankind has their existence in him. The belief is that mankind has their souls in the matter of mother earth, the goddess who provides food so they may develop power from what they consume. Their human existence is twofold—one is a state of blissful unification with Brahman, and the other inhibited by the restraints of impermanence and restrictions in order to obtain peaceful soundness in their being. The people of Hinduism observe rites; however, the gods to whom they bequeath their gifts can make allowances. They believe they will be reincarnated as another creature in the after-life and will be set in a place in accordance to the merits of accumulation in their life.

On the contrary, the gift of salvation in Christianity was already purchased in full by God's begotten Son Jesus. *"For God so loved the world that He gave His only begotten Son, but whosoever believeth in Him should not perish, but have everlasting life"* (John 3:16, KJV). There is no price to pay for this salvation because Jesus paid the price with His precious blood. He did this so mankind could be saved from their

---

[15] The information on the religion of Hinduism is taken from Hendrik M. Vroom's book, <u>Religions and the Truth</u>, (Grand Rapids, Michigan: William B. Eerdmans Publishing Company, 1989), pp. 114-115.

destructive souls. In addition, because God knew the souls of man would need help in finding his way back to Him, He sent His Holy Spirit to guide man on the right path. Therefore, Christianity is not about a religion, but it is about a relationship with God, Who is Love and Liberation.

The Authentic God: Ancient of Days

The God of Christianity is neither comparable nor equivalent to Buddha, Rama or Krishna, Allah or Biame. He is neither a religion of codes, rules or legalistic orders. He is however, the "Authentic God" with many names, one of which is "The Ancient of Days." Another name for the God of Christianity is "The God of Salvation," Who, beyond doubt offers salvation, peace, and love not just to the soul of man, but to man's entire being. He is the One True God of love who is able to convey son-ship while expressing the true satiating reconciliation of His Son, Jesus, to the keen, dark, ambiguous, vacant soul. Lester Summrall, in his book, The Names of God, (New Kensington, PA: Whitaker House, 1982), pp. 28-29, states that the God Who spoke to Moses out of the burning bush was real. He states:

> "Religious hucksters have invaded human society. Fakes, quacks, and charlatans set up false gods, or make false claims about the true God, to make a reputation for themselves and reap a handsome profit. Self-professed healers often demand that people pay them large sums of money before they pray for their victims' healing. Money-grabbing 'gurus' use every sort of gimmick imaginable to reap profits from their ministry. They succeed because man is so desperate to find the one true God, and to follow Him.
>
> The God who spoke to Moses out of the burning bush was real. He said His name is 'I AM,' not 'I am supposed to be' or 'Some people think I am.' God needs no one to make extravagant claims for Him. He doesn't need to be sold, glamorized, or promoted by anyone. He will be worshiped for what He is, not for the image that someone may fabricate of Him."

The God of Christianity, the "Ancient of Days," is not about taking; He is entirely about giving. He is the true living God Who fashioned and framed the worlds into existence with His spoken Word. Daniel 7:9 states, *"I beheld till the thrones were cast down, and the **Ancient of days** did sit, whose garment was white as snow, and the hair of his head like the pure wool: his throne was like the fiery flame, and his wheels as burning fire"* (KJV). Elohim, the Creator of mankind, is omnipotent, omniscient and omnipresent and different from all other gods. There is none like Him and nothing can compare to the God Who was, Who is, and is to come. He is the God Who WAS from the beginning of time, and Who has no END.

He is the only God who offers salvation without having to give him back whatsoever in return to recompense for the value of that redemption. Psalm 68:19-20 declares, *"Blessed be the Lord, who daily loadeth us with benefits, even the God of our salvation. Selah. He that is our God is **the God of salvation**; and unto* GOD *the Lord belong the issues from death"* (KJV). This Salvation is to deliver the benefits of peace, security and love, not just to the yearning soul of man, but to his entire being of spirit, soul and body. I Thessalonians 5:23 declares, *"And the very God of peace sanctify you **wholly**; and I pray God your **whole spirit and soul and body** be preserved blameless unto the coming of our Lord Jesus Christ"* (KJV). Thus, Christianity is not merely a religion like all others, but it is about an intimate relationship between God and His creation whom He made in His own image and in His likeness.

The God of Christianity offers a salvation to man's hurting soul. He is called yet another name, "Jehovah-Shalom," which means the "Lord is Peace." Another title with reference to peace is "The Prince of Peace," given to Jesus, a leader Who brings not conflict and revolt, but peace and righteousness. Isaiah 9:6 states, *"For unto us a child is born, unto us a son is given: and the government shall be upon his shoulder: and his name shall be called Wonderful, Counsellor, The mighty God, The everlasting Father, The **Prince of Peace**"* (KJV). Since He is the Creator of all mankind, He knows them all too well. God knew that man would always have a yearning inside of him to return to the very One Who has always loved him. Until that reconciliation is bonded back together again, man will always live in a lost atmosphere not really knowing or understanding the void they are feeling unless someone leads them to Him.

CHAPTER 6

God is Love: Agape Love Announced

Above all, He is the God of Love, Who is Love. Deuteronomy 7:8-9 decrees, *"But because the* LORD *loved you, and because he would keep the oath which he had sworn unto your fathers, hath the* LORD brought you out with a mighty hand, and redeemed you out of the house of bondmen, from the hand of Pharaoh king of Egypt. *Know therefore that the* LORD *thy God, he is God, the faithful God, which keepeth covenant and mercy with them that love him and keep his commandments to a thousand generations"* (KJV). Because He loved mankind even before the foundations of the world and knew that man's soul had a free will, He made a way for His salvation to be invincible. God made a declaration and announced that He is faithful in keeping His promises to man by fighting to rejoin Himself with His beloved creation. Without God, man is in bondage, just as those Israelites who were in burdensome slavery under the harsh hand of the Pharaoh in Egypt. And, just as God made a way out for the people held in bondage, He continues to provide that same deliverance through His Son Jesus Christ today. His desire is to set every captive soul free and to heal the broken-hearted. Jesus came for the very purpose of saving and seeking the lost and dying world. The prayer of Jesus, while sitting at the right hand of the Father, is that the world may know that just as His Heavenly Father loves Him, He too loves the world. God's intention for mankind is to experience the abundant life once again as they did in the Garden of Eden.

God's *Agape* Love will never give up on man's soul; He will continue to fight the very thing that tries to keep him bound. John Piper, writer for *Desiring God Foundation:* 2013, states that God's salvation could not fail; even if man became disobedient, God would still make a way for His own not to be abandoned. He writes,

"And our confidence is this: as we focus on the great objective work of God, God himself will glorify that work in us by creating faith and assurance and joy and freedom and obedience and power...

God has an unstoppable, undefeatable, invincible purpose to save his people, and the more we dwell on what he has done to infallibly achieve his purpose, the more deep and lively will be our assurance. God loves to glorify the worth of his objective work by making it the basis of our subjective assurance.

God's Invincible Purpose in Our Salvation

We begin where Paul begins in Ephesians 1:3-4. "Blessed be the God and Father of our Lord Jesus Christ, who has blessed us in Christ with every spiritual blessing in the heavenly places, even as he chose us in him before the foundation of the world...

Paul begins by blessing God. He blesses him as one who has blessed us with every blessing that heaven can give. And the first foundation that Paul mentions for this assured fact is that 'God chose us in Christ before the foundation of the world.'

God's Choice of Individuals for Salvation

So that is my first message: God's purpose in the salvation of his people is invincible—it cannot fail—because it is based first not on our choosing God but on God's choosing us. Verse 4: 'He [God] chose us in him [Christ] before the foundation of the world.'

Your salvation did not begin with your choice to believe in Christ—a choice which was real and necessary.

> Your salvation began before the creation of the universe when God planned the history of redemption, ordained the death and the resurrection of his Son, and chose you to be his own through Christ. This is a great objective ground for assurance. And we should consider it deeply."

Furthermore, God's Agape Love is relentless; He will not give up on mankind and will continue to pursue him. God's *Agape* Love will make a difference in the lives of those who receive His love. His love heals the soul of past wounds, resentments, grudges, pride, jealousy and so much more of the emotional pain that man deals with. Merlin R. Carothers, in his book, <u>Power in Praise: How the Spiritual Dynamic of Praise Revolutionizes Lives</u>, (Escondido, CA: Merlin R. Carothers Publishing, 1972) p. 63, states that God is Love and reaches out through that love He possesses—an intense and personal love for each individual in His creation. He states:

> "A love that accepts, approves of, and believes in others, is patient and kind, never selfish or envious, never proud or seeking its own reward or way, not touchy or irritable. It doesn't hold grudges, and doesn't pay attention when it must suffer wrong. A love that is loyal, that believes the best and expects the best, is never glad when someone suffers wrong, but is always happy when truth wins out. Such a love endures without weakening in all circumstances.
>
> This is the kind of love God has for us, and the kind of love He commands that we have for each other. This is the kind of love that heals the wounds of old hurts, casts out fears, melts away resentments and old grudges. This is the kind of love that makes us whole and able to love in return without fear of being rejected or hurt.
>
> This is the love the Greeks called agape, a deliberate, reasoning, intentional, spiritual devotion. This is the love that is a fruit of the Holy Spirit, and when it is fully grown, it draws others to its source- God's love for us in Christ Jesus.
>
> Every one of the gifts and manifestations of the Holy Spirit is given specifically to show God's love and concern for

our every need. God heals because He loves us; He performs miracles because He loves us. God is love. His power reaching out through us is love – a supernatural, divine, intensely personal love for each individual in His creation."

Yes, sometimes this *Agape* Love can be difficult to understand because the logical or natural mind is not familiar or used to functioning in this fashion. Man's soulish ways of love operate with conditions like the loves of *eros*[16], *phileo*[17], *and stergos*[18]. What makes all these other loves different than the *Agape* Love, is that their actions totally connect and operate in the soul part of man, and not in the spirit part of man. Because these different types of "loves" operate in the soul realm, they are restricted and restrained in sharing with others. These are the types of "love" that involve limits, boundaries, conditions and restrictions. These are the types of love that will eventually cause relationships to expire. Charles and Caroline Muir, the authors of Tantra: The Art of Conscious Loving, (San Francisco, California: Mercury House, 1989) pp. 5-6, explain why love is lost, and how the door of passion closes when the familiar becomes all too "familiar." Their book was written with the intention of trying to hoist a couple's bond to an art level called *Tantra*. This method of teaching refers to a system of ancient Hindu secret tomes that impart specific erotic sexual rituals, disciplines, and soul-searching. The focus on this type of philosophical concept is for the couple to experience a spiritual sexual love in their conscious realm which should aid in the ridding of conflicts, which hinder their love. The authors state:

"There's love, and then there's Love. There's passionate love, and then there's love after passion or without passion. The latter has been known, in fact, to be quite cozy and

---

[16] Eros is from the Greek word for "erotic or passionate;" it is a passionate physical and emotional love based on aesthetic pleasure; this is viewed as "romantic love."

[17] Phileo is from the Greek word for "friendship." The best description of this love is found in the close knit relationship between best friends David and Jonathan in the Bible.

[18] Stergos is from the Greek word for "affection" especially between family members or people who connect through familiarity.

satisfying in many ways; but love without passion may also deteriorate into as pale a version of the original as benign tolerance, and there is the risk that it may die completely or turn into resentment or disrespect, or worse.

It is not dispassionate love that we want to discuss. We want to focus on love that is full of passion and heat, love that makes your blood fairly pulse inside you; love that is all the nourishment you need. This is the love that overcomes all obstacles, dissolves time, obsesses you, possesses you, and radiates from you so that people comment on your "glow," and are drawn to you as if by a magnet. This is love that expresses itself sexually as a wonder, the best ever. It is so for both of you—you can't get enough of one another.

Love is not necessarily blind, as Shakespeare claimed, but it is surely an altered state. Physicians tell us that biochemically, love shares a lot of the same exhilarating effects that amphetamines produce. We know that the immune system can be strengthened by it; that white blood cells perform better; and that the production of endorphins increases. We feel terrific!

Part of the answer can be found if we consider passion as a kind of energy that depends on their energy for its survival. When we are in the early passionate stages of a relationship, we expend a lot of energy trying to win one another, enchant, impress, and attract one another. We mentioned that passionate love overcomes obstacles. It is the *energy* required in that overcoming that is most significant. For example, when men and women decide to live together, they eliminate one of the biggest obstacles of all—physical separation—but they don't realize that they are removing something that has contributed to their passion. They need to find a way to compensate for the energy-hole their relationship experiences when they no longer need to overcome the obstacle of living separately. They have created an energy void, and passion suffers for it. The diminution of energy diminishes passion."

On the contrary, the *Agape* Love of God has no limits or boundaries. Mankind does not have to work at finding a way get the attention of God so He can love them, or to compensate for passion being eliminated. His love never fails and never ends towards His beloved creation. His love is for whosoever will receive Him as the Redeemer, Who rekindles the truest and purest love that was tainted by sin. That "energy-hole" that all experience, or will eventually experience at some time in life, is well able to be abundantly filled with the *Agape* Love of God.

It must be made clear that many times when man chooses to remain stubborn in refusing to answer the loving call of his Creator, this will not cause God to stop loving him. His love is unconditional and is not based on the functions of man, or how good he is. Man does not have to exert to win the love of God, or try to accomplish a particular duty in order to try to please Him. God will continue to love mankind regardless of how he behaves. This is why man's logical mind cannot comprehend how deep God's love really is. This is the marvelous *Agape* Love of God! T. D. Jakes, in his book, <u>Intimacy With God</u>, (Tulsa, Oklahoma: Albury Publishing, 2000) pp. 108, 111-112, states that the love of God is not something that our mind can comprehend for it is something that passes man's knowledge. He writes:

"The love of God is not something we can 'know' with our mind. It is something that 'passeth knowledge.' It is beyond our ability to comprehend with our minds...

That's why Paul said, 'I pray that you might know the love of Christ.' This is a love that 'blows the mind' because it's beyond anything we can know. It cannot be compared to anything we grew up with, experienced in that past, are married to, or have given birth to. The love that God has for us is infinitely pure, infinitely accepting, infinitely patient and kind, infinitely generous, infinitely more than any other kind of love. It's so high, you can't get over it. It's so low, you can't get under it. It's so wide, you can't go around it. It's so deep, you can never get to the bottom of it. And what you cannot fathom with your mind, you can never exhaust!"

The *Agape* Love of God is the greatest out of all other loves because it is divine. It is so divine that it is able to transform all the other natural loves that manifest in the soul of man. It will transform the receiving of love into the giving of love, because God is Love, and the Lover of man's soul. C. S. Lewis, in his book, The Four Loves, (New York, NY: Houghton Mifflin Harcourt Publishing, 1960) pp. 131,133-134, gives a profound description of the *Agape* Love of God, which he refers to "Charity." He states:

"But God also transforms our Need-love for one another, and it requires equal transformation. In reality we all need at times, some of us at most times, that Charity from others which, being Love Himself in them, loves the unlovable. But this, though a sort of love we need, is not the sort we want. We want to be loved for our cleverness, beauty, generosity, fairness, usefulness. The first hint that anyone is offering us the highest love of all is a terrible shock. This is so well recognized that spiteful people will pretend to be loving us with Charity precisely because they know that it will wound us. To say to one who expects a renewal of Affection, Friendship, or Eros, 'I forgive you as a Christian' is merely a way of continuing the quarrel. Those who say it are of course lying. But the thing would not be falsely said in order to wound unless, if it were true, it would be wounding…

Thus God, admitted to the human heart, transforms not only Gift-love but Need-love; not only our Need-love of Him, but our Need-love of one another. This is of course not the only thing that can happen. He may come on what seems to us a more dreadful mission and demand that a natural love be totally renounced. A high and terrible vocation, like Abraham's, may constrain a man to turn his back on his own people and his father's house. Eros, directed to a forbidden object, may have to be sacrificed. In such instances, the process, though hard to endure, is easy to understand. What we are more likely to overlook is the necessity for a transformation even when the natural love is our silver to make room for the gold. The natural loves are summoned to become modes of charity while also remaining the natural loves they were.

One sees here at once a sort of echo or rhyme or corollary to the Incarnation itself. And this need not surprise us, for the Author of both is the same. As Christ is perfect God and perfect Man, the natural loves are called to become perfect Charity and also perfect natural loves. As God becomes Man 'Not by conversion of the Godhead into flesh, but by taking of the Manhood into God,' so here; Charity does not dwindle into merely natural love but natural love is taken up into, made the tuned and obedient instrument of, Love Himself."

The Key is to Receive

In addition, God's *Agape* Love not only heals all the pain in the soul, but it also transforms the soul. In order to experience this amazing and awesome love that never fails, one must **receive** The Gift Who is Jesus Christ, the Son of God. Once a person receives the *Agape* Love of God, it transforms man's thinking, the choices he makes, and his emotions. His emotions no longer manifest like an uncontrollable wild fire. The soul of man becomes stable because now the Spirit of God lives on the inside of him. God now dwells in the spirit of man transforming man's soul to become more like Him. As God's love transforms and heals man's once stinging soul, He will then process him and teach him how to give love. Then the giving, receiving, and manifesting of God's love towards others will not be as difficult as before. In another book by T. D. Jakes called, Six Pillars From Ephesians: Loved By God, (Tulsa, Oklahoma: Albury Publishing, 2000) pp. 67-68, Pastor Jakes states that God's Love restores on the inside and causes a person's self-confidence to be edified; all of the emotional sufferings will eventually be appeased. He states:

"We cannot shut off, stop, or in any way diminish God's flow of love toward us. No matter what we do, we cannot cause God to stop loving us.

Nothing can move us from the position of being loved by God.

Nothing can change the way God feels about us.

Nothing can alter the fact that God is going to continue to love us no matter what we do or say.

Receiving God's love heals us on the inside. It causes a person's self-esteem to be built up and emotional hurts to be soothed.

Receiving God's love allows us to feel value, worth, and dignity.

Receiving God's love allows us to respect ourselves.

Receiving God's love motivates us to discipline ourselves.

Receiving God's love gives us the capacity to return His love, love ourselves, and love others.

We are not only chosen by God, but we are eternally, tenderly, unconditionally, and infinitely loved by God. There is no greater blessing, no greater assurance!"

Yes, the key is to receive God's unconditional love that never gives up. This is such a love that gives purpose to the one who thought he had lost all hope. God intervened and made a way to get the attention of mankind so he would not self-destruct. In the process of God's love healing the soul of man, He also makes a way for man to give it away and to share with others as well. Although, he may feel that he is unable to give it away, God gives him the ability to be able to do so. Joyce Meyer, writer of the book, <u>Secrets to Exceptional Living</u>, (New York, NY: Faith Words, 2002) pp. 61-63, states that at first it was difficult for her to love others because she simply did not know how to give that love away. She tells of how she had to first receive God's love, and then she was able to give it away, making her life so much better. She states:

"I could not love others because I had never received God's love for me. For many years I mentally acknowledged the Bible teaching that God loved me, but it was not a reality in my heart. Many Christians experience this. The first step in loving others with God's love is to seek to receive the reality that He loves us.

RECEIVE GOD'S LOVE, THEN GIVE IT AWAY

If we are Christians, if we have received Jesus, God's love is already in us for us to receive ourselves and give to others. The Bible tells us, the love of God is shed abroad in our hearts by the Holy Ghost which is given unto us. Already in us is the ability to love people.

As you begin to receive God's love and love yourself in a balanced way, God's love will begin to heal you emotionally so that you are not insecure and fearful or have a poor self-image. We need to spend a certain period of time in our life to settle those areas.

Then instead of spending our entire life trying to receive healing from the pain of our childhood or other stages in our life, we need to go on...

But God has put gifts in us that He wants us to use, and He wants us to receive His love, His healing and give His love to others rather than just sit around and bleed all our life.

Someone who is wounded doesn't just sit there and bleed. The person does something to stop the blood and clean out the wound so that it will heal. Then the person moves on. Some people may need a year or two, even three, to get their emotional wounds healed so they can move on. Some people may even need five. But they don't need twenty, thirty or forty years to receive healing.

If you don't receive healing from the past emotional wounds, you never become strong enough to deal with fresh wounds that may come your way. I would like to promise you that you can reach a place where you will never get hurt again, but I cannot make that promise, and neither can anyone else. I can, however, promise you that Jesus the Healer is always available to heal every wound, old and new."

God's love is so powerful that it not only transforms the soul of man, but it also transforms the lives of others. The *Agape* Love of God is not an earthly love, but a heavenly love that is so influential that when others witness and experience it themselves, they cannot help but be drawn to it. It is the very remedy that is longed for by the soul of man; it is the very powerful and potent tincture that has been sought for since the genuine relationship was lost by the disobedience of the first Adam. As Jerimiah 31:3-4 states, *"The* LORD *hath appeared of old unto me, saying, Yea, I have loved thee with an everlasting love: therefore with loving kindness have I drawn thee. Again I will build thee, and thou shalt be built, O virgin of Israel: thou shalt again be adorned with thy tabrets, and shalt go forth in the dances of them that make merry"* (KJV).

Man Abandons God—God Abandons Man?

It must be made clear that it was not God Who abandoned mankind, nor was it man that abandoned Him. God knew very well of the possibility of man's failure due to his soul. And the lust of pride, God knew very well already for it had occurred once before in heaven. Even in the Garden of Eden, man was given a government where there had to be order. God's order is and has always been an excellent decree. Without order calamity is unstoppable and the world would be in total ruin. God made instruction for the purpose of keeping the world from destroying itself, but in the present age, man still manages to hurt himself and others. Since man was given freewill in the garden; he made the choice not to listen to God but chose to do what he desired. "His eyes were bigger than his appetite," one man stated. In other words, man saw with his eyes something which looked appealing and pleasant to the eyes. Because it looked good, the woman ate of the forbidden fruit and then gave to her husband. Her husband freely took and thus the dilemma of love was created.

God's Love in the Beginning

It was not meant for the separation of God and man to occur; they were to live in constant communion. It was a perfect love of intimate unity until sin entered in through one man's disobedience. Sin was the culprit that alienated God from man. David and Heather Kopp, in their book, <u>Love Stories God Told: The Great Romances of the Bible</u>, (Eugene, Oregon: Harvest House Publishers, 1998) p. 15, describes the perfect love of two until the eating of the tree of knowledge of good and evil. They state:

> "Adam and Eve's story was the first—and in some ways the last—human experience of perfect love. No marriage would ever again be as simple or beautiful. Whereas in Eden life

had been easy, and romance came as naturally as laughter, now the two lovers had to work at everything, including love.

Sound familiar?

To this day, when we discover ourselves tumbling happily into love, we experience a slice of Eden. Everything seems perfect, the birds are always singing, our hearts thrill. Our beloved miraculously completes us. "You are bone of my bone, flesh of my flesh!' we cry.

But as time passes, we eat from the tree of knowledge. Our eyes are opened to our lover's faults and shortcomings. Soon, work and family stresses further test our feelings and our ideals. Gradually, love, as we once knew it, takes a 'fall.'

But the first love story doesn't end there, and ours didn't either. God did not abandon Adam and Eve, nor they each other. Marriage would never be perfect again, but love would still be possible—and more precious than ever!

And that is the hope that echoes down to us through time. We treasure our glimpses of Eden, but the power of our union reaches far beyond the Garden walls. When the bliss of romance falters, another kind of love promises comfort, forgiveness, healing, and hope. And who could treasure these gifts more than fallen humans?

In the familiar embrace of our beloved, we hear God exclaim again, 'It is good!' And we find new strength to face our world together."

Therefore, God's great love for His own made a way to reconcile Himself with the ones he fearfully and wonderfully created. He is a Brilliant God Who knows the way of mankind; He knew his creation would need help in their soul and for this reason God sent His only begotten Son, Jesus Christ incarnate, born of the Virgin Mary, to fix what the first Adam lost. It was the communion between God and man; it was the loving and intense relationship that was beautiful and beyond breathtaking; it was a love that was awe-inspiring.

The greatest and most awe-inspiring description of the love of God is written by the Apostle Paul in I Corinthians 13: 4-13, when speaking to the Corinthians about seeking the greatest gift of all which is love. He states, *"Love endures long and* is patient and kind; love never is envious *nor* boils over with jealousy, is not boastful *or* vainglorious, does not display itself haughtily. *It is not conceited (arrogant and inflated with pride); it is not rude (unmannerly) and does not act unbecomingly. Love (God's love in us) does not insist on its own rights or* its own way, *for* it is not self-seeking; it is not touchy *or* fretful *or* resentful; it takes no account of the evil done to it [it pays no attention to a suffered wrong]. *It does not rejoice at injustice and unrighteousness but rejoices when right and* truth prevail. *Love bears up under anything and* everything that comes, is ever ready to believe the best of every person, its hopes are fadeless under all circumstances, and it endures everything [without weakening]. *Love never fails [never fades out or becomes obsolete or comes to an end]. As for prophecy (the gift of interpreting the divine will and purpose), it will be fulfilled and pass away; as for tongues, they will be destroyed and* cease; as for knowledge, it will pass away [it will lose its value and be superseded by truth]. *For our knowledge is fragmentary (incomplete and imperfect), and our prophecy (our teaching) is fragmentary (incomplete and imperfect). But when the complete and perfect (total) comes, the incomplete and* imperfect will vanish away (become an*tiquated, void, and superseded). When I was a child, I talked like a child, I thought like a child, I reasoned like a child; now that I have become a man, I am done with childish ways and* have put them aside. *For now, we are looking in a mirror that gives only a dim (blurred) reflection [of reality as in a riddle or enigma], but then [when perfection comes] we shall see in reality and face to face! Now I know in part (imperfectly), but then I shall know and* understand *fully and* clearly, even in the same manner as I have been fully *and* clearly known *and understood [by God]. And so, faith, hope, love abide [faith—conviction and belief respecting man's relation to God and divine things; hope—joyful and confident expectation of eternal salvation; love—true affection for God and man, growing out of God's love for and in us], these three; but the greatest of these is love"* (AMP).

Jesus the Reconciliation

To receive this great love, once again God made a way through His Son Jesus Christ, by offering the free gift already purchased in full by His own blood to cleanse man from the sins of his soul. Since the soul is the place of the mind, will, and emotions, and where the first man, Adam made the choice to disobey God and not hearken to His Voice, God uses the same part of man to receive Him back into his life. Although, the Spirit of God does not inhabit the spirit part of man in his unregenerate state, God, in His Splendid ways, provided His Holy Spirit to convict the world of sin to draw him back to Himself.

Holy Spirit: Courier to Righteousness—Comforter to Contentment

It is the Holy Spirit Who draws mankind to His Son Jesus, Who is the Mediator and the Reconciliation, to bring man in union with his Heavenly Father. It is through Jesus Christ that man can experience and embrace that remarkable relationship that was lost in the garden. Jesus, when speaking to His disciples, declared to them words of how necessary it was for the Holy Spirit to come to the earth to convict the world of sin, and also to help the ones who already believed. It is not only the unsaved and unbelieving world that need help, but even the saints of God sing the blues too. John 16:7- 28 declares, *"However, I am telling you nothing but the truth when I say it is profitable (good, expedient, advantageous) for you that I go away. Because if I do not go away, the Comforter (Counselor, Helper, Advocate, Intercessor, Strengthener, Standby) will not come to you [into close fellowship with you]; but if I go away, I will send Him to you [to be in close fellowship with you]. And when He comes, He will convict and* convince the world *and* bring demonstration to it about sin and about righteousness (uprightness of heart and right standing with God) and about judgment: *About sin, because they do not believe in Me [trust in, rely on, and adhere to Me]; About righteousness (uprightness of heart and right standing with God), because I go to My Father, and you will see Me no longer; About judgment, because the ruler (evil genius, prince) of this world [Satan] is judged and* condemned *and sentence already is passed upon him. I have still many things to say to you, but you are not able to bear them or* to take them upon you *or to grasp them now. But when He, the Spirit of Truth (the Truth-giving Spirit) comes, He will guide you into all the Truth (the whole, full Truth). For He will not speak His own message [on His own authority]; but He will tell whatever He hears [from the Father; He will give the message that has been given to Him], and He will announce and declare to you the things that are to come [that will happen in the future].*

He will honor and glorify Me, because He will take of (receive, draw upon) what is Mine and will reveal (declare, disclose, transmit) it to you. *Everything that the Father has is Mine. That is what I meant when I said that He [the Spirit] will take the things that are Mine and will reveal (declare, disclose, transmit) it to you. In a little while you will no longer see Me, and again after a short while you will see Me. So some of His disciples questioned among themselves, What does He mean when He tells us, In a little while you will no longer see Me, and again after a short while you will see Me, and, Because I go to My Father? What does He mean by a little while? We do not know or* understand what He is talking about. *Jesus knew that they wanted to ask Him, so He said to them, Are you wondering and* inquiring among yourselves what I meant when I said, In a little while you will no longer see Me, and again after a short while you will see Me? I assure you, most solemnly I tell you, that you shall weep and grieve, but the world will rejoice. You will be sorrowful, but your sorrow will be turned into joy. *A woman, when she gives birth to a child, has grief (anguish, agony) because her time has come. But when she has delivered the child, she no longer remembers her pain (trouble, anguish) because she is so glad that a man (a child, a human being) has been born into the world. So for the present you are also in sorrow (in distress and depressed); but I will see you again and [then] your hearts will rejoice, and no one can take from you your joy (gladness, delight). And when that time comes, you will ask nothing of Me [you will need to ask Me no questions]. I assure you, most solemnly I tell you, that My Father will grant you whatever you ask in My Name [as presenting all that I Am]. Up to this time you have not asked a [single] thing in My Name [as presenting all that I Am]; but now ask and keep on asking and you will receive, so that your joy (gladness, delight) may be full and* complete. *I have told you these things in parables (veiled language, allegories, dark sayings); the hour is now coming when I shall no longer speak to you in figures of speech, but I shall tell you about the Father in plain words and* openly (without *reserve*). *At that time you will ask (pray) in My Name; and I am not saying that I will ask the Father on your behalf [for it will be unnecessary].* **For the Father Himself [tenderly] loves you** because you have loved Me and have believed that I came out from the Father. I came out from the Father and have come into the world; again, I am leaving the world and going to the Father" (AMP).

Even today, God, in His great love and mercy, patiently waits for the return of His own. He waits like the father in the account of the prodigal son who journeyed to a far country leaving the house where he lacked nothing. When the son came to his senses, eventually making his way home to the house of his father, he humbly repented and reunited with his father who had always been there. He will never force man to serve Him; He gives every person free will—the power to make choices on their own. The *Agape* Love of God is the Answer for the yearning soul of man; He is the Answer to man's spirit, for this is the part that becomes reconciled when man chooses to receive God through His Son, Jesus, to enter once again in his life. C. S. Lewis, in his book, <u>Mere Christianity: What One Must Believe To Be A Christian</u>, (New York, NY: Macmillan Publishing Co., Inc., 1943) pp. 51-52, shares his thoughts on why man does not turn to their Savior so hastily. He writes:

> "Christians, then, believe that an evil power has made himself for the present the Prince of the World and, of course, that raises problems. Is this state of affair in accordance with God's will or not? If it is, He is a strange God, you will say: and if it is not, how can anything happen contrary to the will of a being with absolute power?
>
> But anyone who has been in authority knows how a thing can be in accordance with your will in one way and not in another. It may be quite sensible for a mother to say to the children, 'I'm not going to go and make you tidy on your own.' Then she goes up one night and finds the Teddy bear and the ink and the French Grammar all lying in the grate. That is against her will. She would prefer the children to be tidy. But on the other hand, it is her will which has left the children free to be untidy. The same thing arises in any regiment, or trade union, or school. You make a thing voluntary and then half the people do not do it. That is not what you willed, but your will has made it possible."

In addition, He is the God who the Apostle Peter states as, *"Neither is there salvation in any other; for there is none other name under heaven given among men, whereby we must be saved"* (Acts 4:12, KJV). Thus, salvation cannot come from any other god or religion except through the Son of God which is referred to by the apostles, John and Peter. The emphasis of the apostles in the Bible is that God loves His creation so passionately that He desires to bring salvation to all who will receive His love. It is the God who the Apostle John speaks about while on the Island of Patmos, recorded in the book of Revelation 21:5-7 which states, *"And he that sat upon the throne said, Behold, I make all things new. And he said unto me, Write: for these words are true and faithful. And he said unto me, It is done. **I am Alpha and Omega, the beginning and the end. I will give unto him that is athirst of the fountain of the water of life freely.** He that overcometh shall inherit all things; and I will be his God, and he shall be my son"* (KJV). Again, He is mentioned as the God of love who denotes salvation by making all things new and delivering a satisfaction quenching of the thirsty soul. To those that surmount, He gives an inheritance of all things and a title called "son."

God so Loved, to Die and to Rise

God is *Agape* Love, the overwhelming love of grace, mercy and kindness. T. D. Jakes, author of the book, <u>The Lady, Her Lover, and Her Lord</u>, (New York, NY: G. P. Putnam's Sons Publishers, 1998), pp. 9-10, briefly describes how powerful the different types of love are and the effects of each, but then describes how much more intense the Love of God is Who longs to bring salvation to the world. He writes:

> "Love—what a word! It is a small word possessing only four letters, but it is loaded to the brim with every imaginable feeling. The Greeks have many words to describe the multifaceted concept of love. They divide the *agape* kind of love from the *philia* kind of love. The agape describes the divine, while the *philia* describes the brotherly affection between siblings and shared among humans. They use the word *eros*—from which we get the word erotic—to describe the abstract feelings of the heart, but to have only one word to describe all the types and levels of feelings, a

word that means different things to different people—well, we often fail to describe the variety or the intensity of the intoxicating impact of the love feeling.

Love is to life what a scent is to a rose. It is the spice of life, and it adorns life as clouds decorate the skies. Many women have tasted the nectar of romance. Many men have swayed beneath the influence of the memory of a special moment shared with that special someone. Even the aged see youth rekindled in the emblazoned moments of affection and the displayed admission of concern. From the cooing sound of a contented baby, to the calm breathing of an aged grandmother, there is the constant need for and appreciation of affections that affect the ordinary and transform the mediocre. Yes, love is the elixir of the soul. It is a common denominator, something we all need regardless of our varied perspectives or vicissitudes of life. Whether love is communicated through a soft touch or a moistened eye, it is the message that we need. The method is immaterial in comparison to the magnitude of the message itself.

There is no drug that can compare with the intense, passionate feelings that are aflame when the heart is in love. It is love that causes the senses to heighten. It is love that causes the heart to pump honey to the soul and sedation to the mind. It is the sweet taste of the honeycomb that satisfies the taste buds of the soul. Without love, life tastes bland, and success is empty.

What can compete with love? It has kept the sick man alive and made the well man feel sick. It is love that gives us courage and yet love that makes us afraid. It weakens the mighty and strengthens the feeble. It is the most intoxicating feeling that any of us will ever have the privilege of experiencing. If it is given to the worthy, it is reciprocated and fruitful. If it is invested on the empty opportunist, it can create a pain that nauseates the soul and afflicts the mind. It can make an average person deem extraordinary. It has the capabilities to alter our perceptions and heighten our vulnerability. It is love that made Christ die and still that same love that made him arise from the grave."

Without a doubt, every soul has the longing to love and to be loved by that special someone. However, the love that is the authentic cure that comes from God is not the same kind of love that causes simple sweet men and women to become crazy insane maniacs ready to hurt others, wanting to cause others to feel the same grief they feel, to experience the same hurt they feel. The very thing that the lost and oppressed soul longs for is to genuinely love, knowing and having faith in that person, that from one day to the next they will not get up and leave. The crying and oppressed have experienced this type of love many times; now they long for that divine love like no other. This is first and foremost the most basic need emotionally that is genuinely desired by all. Gary Chapman, writer of the book, The Five Love Languages, (Chicago, IL: Northfield Publishing, 1992), p. 35, expresses the kind of **real love** that is sought after and gives the statistics of failed marriages in this country. He writes,

> "Presently 40 percent of first marriages in this country end in divorce. Sixty percent of second marriages and 75 percent of third marriages end the same way. Apparently, the prospect of a happier marriage the second and third time around is not substantial.
>
> Research seems to indicate that there is a third and better alternative: we can recognize the in-love experience for what it was—a temporary emotional high—and now pursue "real love" with our spouse. That kind of love is emotional in nature but not obsessional. It is a love that unites reason and emotion. It involves an act of the will and requires discipline, and it recognizes the need for personal growth. Our most basic emotional need is not to fall in love but to be genuinely loved by another, to know a love that grows out of reason and choice, not instinct. I need to be loved by someone who chooses to love me, who sees in me something worth loving.
>
> This kind of love requires effort and discipline. It is the choice to expend energy in an effort to benefit the other person, knowing that if his or her life is enriched by your effort, you too will find a sense of satisfaction—the

satisfaction of having genuinely loved another. It does not require the euphoria of the "in love" experience. In fact, true love cannot begin until the "in love" experience has run its course."

Uniquely, this path which is spoken above is the course that leads to the Agape Love of God. No one will ever be able to be comforted from the turmoil that is experienced in the soul unless he first allows the "in love" progression to surrender to God's true love. This true love will always possess a genuine peace and satisfaction that only comes from God.

CHAPTER 7

"What, There is No God?"

The atheist will pompously ask "What is this *Agape* Love of God all about, and what can He offer that other religions cannot?" Is this so called *"Agape* Love" the answer to the lost soul wishing to fill his heavy disposition? The statement in I John 4:9 declares, *"In this was manifested the love of God toward us, because that God sent his only begotten Son into the world, that we might live through him"* (KJV). Life is meant to be lived in an excellent and exceptional way and it is only by receiving this *"Agape* Love" that many are able to love life to the fullest. As has been stated earlier, many atheists have come to find the truth that leads them to the salvation of Jesus. They have come to the conclusion in their lives that not even man's intelligence can figure out the love, peace, security and everything else God offers unless they receive the Holy Spirit's voice to draw them back to their Creator. They find that God is the Answer that every soul needs in order to live life to the fullest. The same writer also declares that through this "Son of God," the despairing soul could find true life by receiving the Son of God Who gives abundant life[19].

---

[19] This is referring to the writing of the Apostle John approximately in A.D. 90. He speaks of Jesus being the true shepherd to his sheep, a metaphor referring to His people. He refers to "abundant life" as salvation, nourishment, healing and much more. It reads as, *"The thief does not come except to steal, and to kill, and to destroy. I have come that they may have life, and that they may have it more abundantly"* (John 10:10, NKJV).

The Doubter Constantly Questions

Thus, another journey begins towards the goal of possessing a soothing soul with the sanguinity to escort visible or tangible evidence about a God who claims to love the world, but whose actions show forth otherwise. One wonders about this love of God and its limits towards people when all types of ministers in diverse religions all claim to hold the truth but yet have dissimilar veracities. The general sermons ministers preach are about God's love that saves the souls of men who receive Him but forsakes those sinners who reject Him. *If He is such a god of love who offers His love, why then, would He forsake those He created?* The dearth of reality can bear the exhibition of an unsound soul that restricts a life to dullness, incorporating an irresolute pursuit for existing. When there are unknown facts about the Ultimate Divinity's demeanor, and when those facts are not fully understood at first glance of the Holy Scriptures, anxiety can constrain the quality of life to a misdirected wandering wilderness of the mind.

At first examination of the translation of the King James Version of the Holy Bible by the eminent King James I of England in the 17th Century, it is obvious that God is not merely love. There is far more to Him than what the average Sunday school teacher leads one to believe. He/she either passively embeds in the minds of men that the God of love cannot annihilate those who live corruptly, or, he/she extremely entrenches in the sad truth-seeker that God's wrath will someday destroy all wicked sinners, who choose not to repent and receive His love of salvation, with the unbearable fires and brimstone of Hell which He, let us forget not, created Himself. If God so loves the world, why would he bring a flood to destroy the earth and why would he show forth His wrath on the people of Sodom and Gomorrah? While the need for love continues to fatigue the bewildered soul, the search for the One, who is able to escort that enlightened love, remains.

The unabridged truth of existence is what many desire of this so called, "Higher Power," Who is to escort salvation while permeating His love and peace in the soul realm of mankind because *He first loves them*. However, information by many expounds that there is a flip side to the character of this "Living Divinity" that has been known to forsake those sinners who reject Him. The search for salvation incorporating love, with the uncertainty of that truth which voids the souls of men displaying peculiar actions, brings forth the labeling upon them of emotionally unstable. Others are labeled eccentric, emotionally unstable, weird, crazy and mentally ill whose actions manifest in bizarre ways due to the misconceptions of this "Divine Architect" of life itself. The quest for knowledge about the Supreme Creator of the universe bridles the souls of men to the point of a disillusioned life. The prison of the cryptic soul has entombed them in a world of criticism where hostilities reside; they are lost in a dark world of the oxymoron, the "living-dead," yearning for the certainty of emancipation that they might grasp the radiance of rest, instead of their discernible destiny. The search for reality shall linger with confidence in the salvation provided by this "Superior Sovereignty of Love," Who will potentially generate tranquility to the perplexed.

Could it possibly be, as the Apostle Paul noted in the writings to the Corinthians in A.D. 56, that those who are lost are the very ones who are hidden to the gospel of Jesus? Are the minds of men truly blinded by the god of this world, who believe not in the glorious light of Christ? Is this so called "Christ" to bring clarity to these who are bound when they believe?[20] Could it possibly be this simple for the lost soul to be set free, just by believing that there is a true and living God Who created the universe? Perhaps this is the reason for the emptiness in the lives of so many who are absent to the joys of the world, those who question *the existence of God* and *the origin of love*. For the one who continues to question the reality of a Divine Creator, the expedition proceeds; only time and investigation can provide the sound mind that is desired by the restricted soul and deliver it from the chains of not knowing. There must be an obtainable answer for the misapprehensions of life which merely convey melancholia.

---

[20] The Second Epistle of Paul, the Apostle, to the Corinthian church was written in A.D. 56; they are urged to live holy lives, repent of their past sins, and to reunite themselves to each other, due to divisions. He notes that the god of this world has blinded the minds of unbelievers; these remain blind unless they believe in the light of the gospel of Jesus Christ. This passage is found in 2 Corinthians 4:3-4 in the King James Version of the Holy Bible.

The Fool says, "There is No God!"

According to the writer of Psalms, the one who declares, "There is no God," is a fool and therefore, the source for the lack of his own understanding. This fool is also filled with corruption and engaged in iniquity that can do no good in life.[21] This declaration includes the scattering of bones and open shame to the one who positions himself against God; these are strong arguments pertaining to the one who does not believe in God.

Dr. Sigmund Freud's Theory on God and Love

Dr. Sigmund Freud, founder of psychoanalysis, would most definitely fit this description then. Of course, there are those that would not agree with the writings of the Holy Bible, and they would never call Dr. Freud a fool. Today, Freud's scientific contributions are categorized on the same level as Einstein's by historians. He is recognized as one of the utmost physicians in history and appeared on the cover of *Time Magazine* on an issue regarding the greatest scientific minds of the century. His views on the existence of God and love were no secret; he showed no shame in discussing his feeling about the countless majorities of humans who actually believed in what he called, "an idealized superman" in the sky. He referred to himself as an atheist, a godless man, an infidel, and an unbeliever. Dr. Armand M. Nicholi, Jr., author of the book, The Question of God, (New York, NY: Free Press Publishing, 2002), pp. 37-38, describes Sigmund Freud's attitudes regarding his beliefs on an intelligence beyond the universe. He writes:

> "In his philosophical writings Freud divides all people not into psychiatric categories, but into 'believers' and 'unbelievers.' Under unbelievers he includes all those who call themselves materialists, seekers, skeptics, agnostics,

---

21 This passage is taken from the King James Version of the Holy Bible. Psalm 53:1-3, 5 states, *"The fool hath said in his heart, There is no God. Corrupt are they, and have done abominable iniquity: there is none that doeth good. 2 God looked down from heaven upon the children of men, to see if there were any that did understand, that did seek God. 3 Every one of them is gone back: they are altogether become filthy; there is none that doeth good, no, not one...5 for God hath scattered the bones of him that encampeth against thee: thou hast put them to shame, because God hath despised them."*

and atheists; under believers he includes a spectrum from all those who merely give intellectual assent to some kind of Supernatural Being to those, like Lewis,[22] who describe a transforming spiritual experience that revolutionizes their lives and literally makes them into 'new creatures.'

Freud calls his worldview 'scientific,' because of its premise that knowledge comes only from research. Of course, this basic premise cannot itself be based on scientific research. Rather, it is a philosophical assumption that cannot be proven. One can only *assume* that all knowledge comes from 'research' and that 'no knowledge' comes 'from revelation.'

Freud appears to realize that logically one cannot prove a negative—one cannot *prove* that God does not exist. The only real defense of his worldview is to discredit its alternative. Thus, Freud undertook a systematic and sustained attack on the spiritual worldview. He attacked it with sledgehammer blows. He wrote that the 'tales of miracles ... contradicted everything that had been taught by sober observation and betrayed too clearly the influence of the activity of the human imagination.' He asserted that the Scriptures 'are full of contradictions, revisions and falsifications'; he said no intelligent person can accept the 'absurdities' or 'fairy tales' of believers.

Freud wrote that the doctrines of religion 'bear the imprint of the times in which they arose, the ignorant times of the childhood of humanity,' that the specific doctrine that 'the universe was created by a being resembling a man, but magnified in every respect...an idealized superman... reflects the gross ignorance of primitive peoples.'

He described the spiritual worldview as 'distorting the picture of the real world in a delusional manner...and... forcibly fixing [people] in a state of psychical infantilism.' He wrote that 'the religions of mankind must be classed among the mass delusions,' and he referred to religion as 'the

---

[22] Dr. Armand M. Nicholi, Jr. is referring to C. S. Lewis, Oxford don, literary critic, author and brilliant scholar, whose popular works sold millions of copies. His success as a writer occurred after his change of worldviews from atheist to believer.

universal obsessional neurosis of humanity.' He wondered if 'Jesus Christ ... is not a part of mythology' or merely 'an ordinary deluded creature.' In a letter to Oskar Pfister, a friend and clergyman, Freud referred to the teachings of Jesus as 'psychologically impossible and useless for our lives' and concluded, 'I attach no value to the 'imitation of Christ.' Freud refers here to the famous, influential book *The Imitation of Christ*, believed to have been written by Thomas A. Kempis between 1390 and 1440, encouraging readers to follow the example of Jesus Christ in self-denial and in love for others."

As was stated earlier, according to the writer of Psalms, the supposition declares Dr. Sigmund Freud, the legendary and prominent earthly psychologist, who positions himself against the existence of God, a fool; the writer augments that in no way could this fool accomplish good since he commits abominable iniquity whose heart is filled with corruption. Contrary views are evident regarding this man who forms the theory of psychoanalysis, who demonstrates academic brilliance, and is described as "one of the most discussed scientists" who set the entire world, till this day to diagnose others, thereby exhausting psychological terminology in speaking of others. While thriving in his career, he shows no shame in sharing his contemplations on the subject of the existence of God and love and demonstrates no humiliation in pronouncing his credence of God as juvenile and external to realism, and ended up establishing him a fool.

Dr. Sigmund Freud affirmed the truth of the Word of God when it speaks of a reprobate mind not receiving salvation, by his indignation towards God and insolent arguments as to the existence of God and love. The profound question is, "What becomes of those who do not believe in God's reality which involves love; what redemption are they not included in?" Could it possibly be true that one who does not believe and confess that Jesus is the Son of God,[23] is not saved? From

---

23 This is referring to the verse found in Romans 10:9 of the New King James Version of the Bible; this was written in A.D. 57 by the Apostle Paul to the Romans, who, like C. S. Lewis, was converted to Christianity after an encounter of blindness and an experience with the Lord in a supernatural way. He wrote, *"That if thou shalt confess with thy mouth the Lord Jesus, and shalt believe in thine heart that God hath raised him from the dead, thou shalt be saved."*

whom or what would this person not be saved, and would this so called "salvation" involve life here on earth or in eternity, or both? Further enquiry on Dr. Freud's life may bring clarification to what exactly this "salvation" is, and perhaps provide an inkling to the mind yearning to recognize the fate of the one who embraces no acceptance in the credibility of God's presence. A further analysis of the Holy Scripture and the outcome of the life of the legendary and reprobate Sigmund Freud, will enhance the measure of correlation, further explaining his unclear thoughts on salvation.

The Apostle Paul, in writing to the church in Rome, in A.D. 57, anticipated the congregation to understand God's plan of salvation, to receive it and to experience a life of harmony that would follow. He confesses that they are ignorant of God's righteousness and seek to establish their own righteousness by performing works of the Mosaic Law by being religious—dutiful works to institute their redemption. He fervently delivers a detailed message on the true meaning of salvation, he writes, *"Brethren, my heart's desire and prayer to God for Israel is, that they might be saved. For I bear them record that they have a zeal of God, but not according to knowledge. For they being ignorant of God's righteousness, and going about to establish their own righteousness, have not submitted themselves unto the righteousness of God. For Christ is the end of the law for righteousness to every one that believeth. For Moses describeth the righteousness which is of the law, That the man which doeth those things shall live by them. But the righteousness which is of faith speaketh on this wise, Say not in thine heart, Who shall ascend into heaven? (that is, to bring Christ down from above:) Or, Who shall descend into the deep? (that is, to bring up Christ again from the dead.) But what saith it? The word is nigh thee, even in thy mouth, and in thy heart: that is, the word of faith, which we preach; That if thou shalt confess with thy mouth the Lord Jesus, and shalt believe in thine heart that God hath raised him from the dead, thou shalt be saved. For with the **heart** man believeth unto righteousness; and with the **mouth confession** is made unto **salvation**. For the scripture saith, Whosoever believeth on him shall not be ashamed. For there is no difference between the Jew and the Greek: for the same Lord over all is rich unto all that call upon him. For whosoever shall call upon the name of the Lord shall be saved"* (Romans 10:1-13, NKJV).

The Meaning of Salvation

Upon detailed research of the word, "salvation," it is expounded that the Greek word translated is **sōtēría** which means, *God's rescue which delivers believers out of destruction and into His safety.* It also expresses deliverance from wrath from the power of sin. According to *Strong's Concordance of Greek and Hebrew Words*, **sōtēría (salvation)** is defined as, *welfare, prosperity, deliverance, preservation, salvation, safety.* The Apostle Paul clearly states that **sōtēría** is obtained by confessing with the mouth—speaking or voicing, and believing with the heart, that God has raised Jesus from the dead. In addition, **sōtēría** is for *all*, which he articulates with the word, "whosoever," which includes all races and gender of persons who call on the name of the Lord. By one's admittance of the existence of God, and His salvation, God conveys deliverance from the power of sin. Thus, if God's salvation ushers in benefits and blessings to the one who chooses to accept His righteousness by faith, and not by religious works, then the same must be true to the one who chooses to reject God's salvation, consequently remaining under the law of the power of one's own sin.

According to the meaning of the term "salvation," and the declaration given to the church in Rome by the Apostle Paul concerning those establishing their own righteousness, Dr. Sigmund Freud fits a perfect description of that soul who would not experience the salvation of God, unless he came to a position of confessing with his mouth and believing in his heart that God raised Jesus Christ from the dead. This salvation would include benefits that are God's blessing, welfare, prosperity, deliverance and preservation. This preservation is the same expression which the writer of Psalms speaks of; he states: *"Because you have made the Lord your refuge, and the Most High your dwelling place, There shall no evil befall you, nor any plague or calamity come near your tent. For He will give His angels [especial] charge over you to accompany and defend and **preserve** you in all your ways [of obedience and service]. They shall bear you up on their hands, lest you dash your foot against a stone You shall tread upon the lion and adder; the young lion and the serpent shall you trample underfoot. Because he has set his love upon Me, therefore will I deliver him; I will set him on high, because he knows and understands My name [has a personal knowledge of My mercy, love, and* *kindness—trusts and relies on Me, knowing I will never forsake him, no, never]. He shall call upon Me, and I will answer him; I will be with him in trouble, I will deliver him and honor him. With long life will I satisfy him and show him My salvation"* (Psalms 91:9-16, AMP).

Due to Dr. Freud's pronouncements in his dogmas regarding this, "superman in the sky," he would not be an individual experiencing salvation of preservation. Because he chose to reject the refuge of the Lord as his dwelling place, he would not be subject to sheltering from plague or calamity, he would not likewise experience the benefits of God's angels accompanying and defending him; furthermore, the doctor's own confessions indicate that he would not face deliverance from trouble, honor and satisfaction of long life. The congruence of the last days of Dr. Sigmund Freud's life appear to prove that God's Word is valid. Freud experienced a lengthy and agonizing process of dying from esophageal cancer. Although Freud made extreme declarations regarding the realm of the spirit during the last years of his life, he remains faithful to his own standpoint on God's existence. George Prochnik, writer of the book, Putnam Camp, (New York, NY: Other Press Publishing, 2006), pp. 387-388, shares how Freud confesses to have a secret inclination toward the miraculous. He states:

"Whatever philosophical validation the approach of mortality might have tendered, Freud's stoicism in the face of a prolonged, excruciating process of dying was extraordinary. One of his operations triggered an infection in the Eustachian tubes that led to deafness in his right ear. The cannibalization of his mouth by the cancer and consequent operations to excise it eventually necessitated the installation of a prosthetic palate and jaw. The prosthesis never properly fit; it chafed at the sores on his mouth, lacerating his bleeding ulcers even as it distorted his speech. It was a punishment worthy of Freud's beloved Greek myths for the original analyst to be losing both his powers of hearing and of utterance. Near the end, the cancer consumed the inside of his cheek and kept on spreading, protruding through to the surface of his face.

And still Freud did not betray an urge to valorize or sentimentalize his suffering. His tone in referring to his sickness was alternately sardonic (he described the cancer as 'my dear old carcinoma') and analytic (in the last months of his life he wrote Marie Bonaparte to record the psychological sensations associated with the action of radium in his body).

Yet, there was one arena in which the advent of mortality may have pushed Freud's perspective away from the Lethe-lapped bank of classical disdain: the realm of the spirit. On his 75th birthday, in 1931, he told the Chief Rabbi of Vienna, 'In some place in my soul, in a very hidden corner, I am a fanatical Jew.' In 1933, in a letter to a friend, Freud confessed, 'It may be that I too have a secret inclination toward the miraculous.' The fact that he devoted his last years to a study of religion, *Moses and Monotheism*, even in a subversive sense, indicates the degree to which the metaphysical subjects that Putnam[24] had pressed on him had come to occupy Freud in his final years. Nothing would have moved Putnam more than Freud's twilight concern with the unknown, which he'd ostensibly avoided for so much of his life. Putnam would have felt their friendship at last opening to the eternal universe in which the men could find their true, common home."

Although, Dr. Sigmund Freud may have come to a point in believing in the supernatural world and having an "inclination of the miraculous," it is not the same as confessing with the mouth and believing in the heart that God raised Jesus from the dead. He did however, one day, say the word, "*der liebe Gott*," in German, which translates into the word "God" in English, but who would know which god he refers to? Confirmation of his ungodly beliefs during his last years proves that Freud struggled in his soul realm, perhaps almost

---

[24] James Jackson Putnam, was a renowned American psychologist, who shared opposing views and pretensions on human nature with Sigmund Freud; although differences in views, both developed a prolific association with each other.

believing but not relatively. If he perhaps did arrive at a place where he did believe in God, the question is: Would this esteemed man be able to swallow up his pride and tell another soul?

It is acknowledged, nevertheless, that Dr. Sigmund Freud did suffer in his last years with cancer eating away at his life, his arrogance allowing him to call the killer of his spirit, soul and body his "friend." He manifests no evidence or witness of the salvation of God in his life, only the bizarre superstitions about his own death. He admits the attacks and the obsession of the fear of dying, which he often dreamt about. This extreme suffering likewise led Dr. Freud toward thoughts of ending his own life at times, as Dr. Armand M. Nicholi[25] adds.

Dr. Armand mentions how Freud was tremendously anxious of the terrors of eternal emptiness but still stuck with his position in what he believed or did not believe. Furthermore, he was afraid of the suffering he would have to endure; it was reported that Freud asked one of his physicians to aid him in departing from this world with decency if he experienced suffering with his illness. For the concern of Dr. Freud committing suicide, his diagnosis of cancer was kept from him; it was said that when he found out of his diagnosis he felt betrayed. One may wonder if Dr. Freud was mentally ill himself, or if everything he had gone through in his life drew him to this point of sorrow.

Sigmund Freud died by euthanasia on September 22, 1939. The day before his death, he chose a book to read from his library entitled *The Fatal Skin* by Honore de Balzac, which tells the story of a young man with a desire for fame, fortune and glory but sees himself a letdown and contemplates suicide. This young man meets the devil who makes a pact with him promising him to give him everything he wishes; as part of this deal, the young man must take on the skin of a wild ass but with every request he makes, his skin will shrink and his life will be shortened. He is cautioned by the devil, that to desire, or to wish for much, would devour him. Was Freud comparing his life to the young man's life in this story? Could he have made a pact with the devil himself in return for all the fame and glory he received while living on this earth?

[25] In reference, once again, to Dr. Armand's book entitled, The Question of God, (New York, NY: Free Press Publishing, 2002), pp. 222, 226-230.

It is ironic how Dr. Freud, founder of psychoanalysis, was known for the diagnosis for many of the so called "mentally ill," when he himself demonstrates struggles throughout his life of emptiness and sorrow. Of course, he never made a confession to believing in the existence of God and His love towards humanity; instead the "distinguished doctor" made a mockery of God boasting his own accomplishments. In reference to the "Love of God towards humanity," it is nonexistent according to Freud's own philosophy; if there is no God, there is no love of God. As the writers of Psalms and Romans clarify, it is only through confession and believing in Jesus Christ, the Son of God, Who is love, who gives the gift of salvation to all who accept. "Love is the Goal," according to Jay E. Adams, author of the book, Competent to Counseling, (Grand Rapids, Michigan: Zondervan, 1970), pp. 54-55; he states:

> "Love is precisely man's problem, however, How can sinful man love? Since the fall, in which Adam's sin led to a guilty conscience, hypocrisy, and doubt, it has been impossible for natural men to keep their hearts pure, their consciences good, or their faith unhypocritical. All are born with a warped sinful nature that vitiates any such possibility. And yet love depends upon these very qualities. That is why Paul conditioned love upon the solution to these problems (note: 'love from,' i.e., 'which issues from'). God's authoritative instruction through the ministry of his Word, spoken publicly (from the pulpit) or privately (in counseling), is the Holy Spirit's means of producing love in the believer.
>
> The overarching purpose of preaching and counseling is God's glory. But the underneath side of that splendid rainbow is love. A simple biblical definition of love is: The fulfillment of God's commandments. Love is a responsible relationship to God and to man. Love is a relationship conditioned upon responsibility, that is, responsible observance of the commandment of God. The work of preaching and counseling, when blessed by the Holy Spirit, enables men through the gospel and God's sanctifying Word to become pure in heart, to have peaceful consciences, and to trust God sincerely."

An enabling through the gospel, sanctification through God's Word, purity in heart and a peaceful conscience are definitely satisfactions from God's salvation that Dr. Sigmund did not experience. Certainly not acknowledging the Ultimate Creator led him on the pathway of his own fate. Jay Adams gives the answer to why a person suffers from sickness the majority of the time and why this will eventually lead to death if not dealt with. In his assessment he refers to Proverbs 28:13 concisely when counseling those dealing with misery, defeat and ruin. He continues to state:

> "He who conceals his transgressions will not prosper: but he who confesses and forsakes them will obtain mercy.
>
> Those words are straight forward and simple. There is nothing obtuse about them; they say exactly what they mean and mean precisely what they say. God's remedy for man's problems is confession. The concealing of transgressions brings misery, defeat and ruin but the confession and forsaking of sin will bring merciful pardon and relief.
>
> James 5:14 was referred to in an earlier chapter. There can be no doubt that James taught that there is a possibility that sickness may stem from sin. James directed Christians who become sick to 'call for the elders of the church.' This scriptural provision puts the organized church of Jesus Christ squarely in the business of working with those who are sick because of sin. The work of the officers of the church cannot be handed over to psychiatrists on the basis that such persons are 'mentally ill.' Psychiatry has no means for curing *hamartiagenic*[26] sickness. The church must not cower before the threats of psychiatrists who have usurped her territory and now declare that she may not repossess it...
>
> The beneficial effects of righteous living are consistently noted in the Scriptures. References abound in the book of Proverbs. Proverbs 3:1, 2 reads:

---

[26] All sicknesses are a result from the fall of Adam in an indirect sense. *Hamartiagenic* sickness is illness caused by sin and there are certain sins which are the definite outcome of many sicknesses.

My son, do not forget my teaching; let your heart keep my commandments; for length of days and years of life, full of peace, will they add to you (Berkeley Translation).

The proverb says that **long life and peace of mind come through keeping God's commandments.**" Ibid., 105, 122-123.

Mr. Adams does make a strong point in the connection to sickness caused by mental ailment with the sickness associated from the disobedience to God's Word. If the soul of man is in disarray, this will most likely cause disarray of the body bringing about sickness of all kinds. This is why the writer of third John declares, *"Beloved, I wish above all things that thou mayest prosper and be in health, even as thy soul prospereth."* (3 John 2:2, KJV). See, the soul, or the mind, will and emotions of man, must be healthy in order for the body to be healthy. In the same way, if the soul is sick, then most likely the body will be sick, or become sick, if the soul of man is left unattended. Thus, a hurting soul, or even a guilty conscience of sin, could cause grave damage; it is having a sound mind, with no guilty conscience that conveys peace in one's life and delivers contentment and happy living.

Evidence proves there is a correlation between the Holy Scripture and man's demeanor. The life of the prominent Jewish doctor, who becomes the founder of psychoanalysis, flamboyantly declares his beliefs and demonstrates no disgrace in insulting questions to the reality of God and love. His notion remains resilient until infirmity literally binds him, forbidding articulation about God any longer. Like his patients, his soul becomes confined to the pondering of the supernatural life of the miraculous. His expressions of theories which launch infamously are now the identical lexes which establish his own destiny of agony, consenting no occasion for the existence of God's Love to provide salvation to his lost soul.

William Shakespeare, the great English poet of the 17th Century, positions the demand of forbidden love in his play *Romeo and Juliet*, in which Juliet asks the question, "What's in a name? That which we call a rose by any other name would smell as sweet." She conflicts[27] that it is not the name that holds importance but rather what things are. However, according to Christian faith and God, names are extremely valuable, for they are representatives of the significant purpose of actions, whether referring to persons, places or things. In this case, it is His very name, or names, which communicate His nature, character and commitments towards mankind. Unlike Shakespeare's forbidden love scene, God's heart of love is in no way forbidden to anyone. His love is the very reason He creates man and His names tell Who He is.

According to the Bible, one of the names of God is "love" which began in heaven and this type of love cannot be formed or duplicated by any other god. It is a value of love that comprehends no limits or boundaries. The strength of His love is relenting even so that He continues to fight to win the very ones He created; His desire is to reconcile with His beloved children which the god of this world blinds with the idea that there is something far better for man that God is not revealing. Although, the first beings believed the lies of God's enemy, their Creator continued to love them; His love was not, and still is not, based on man's mistakes or failures. It is His goodness and the unconditional love in which He operates, that He hopes will draw His creation to Himself once again. Ben Coblentz, author of the book, Born to Love, (Berlin, Ohio: TGS International, 1993), p. 33, describes His love as, "not of this world." He also comments how God's love is so "wonderful" and "greater and better than our minds can imagine." He writes:

> "God's love surpasses everything that we have been able to compare it with. It surpasses every challenge. It is even greater and better than our minds can imagine because of how it affects our lives. It is so satisfying. It is so fulfilling. It is so blessed to know that our all-wise, almighty heavenly Father has a heart filled with love and compassion for us. It gives us such a relaxed, deep-settled peace within. It gives us the desire to serve Him. It gives us the courage to trust

---

[27] In William Shakespeare's Play, *Romeo and Juliet*; Juliet argues the question of a name (in Act II, Scene 2). The line refers to her forbidden lover, Romeo, who belongs to the house of Montague, her family's rival, which implies that his name does not matter so they can be together.

Him. A desire to just simply be His. His for service. His for fellowship. His to love and share. We need not be ashamed to identify with Him because there is nothing more blessed and wonderful. Awakening to God's wonderful love will usher in a joyous, rewarding fulfillment."

Yes, God's *Agape* Love is the very remedy man diligently seeks, it is the joyous, rewarding fulfillment the soul of man experiences when he has willed to receive God in his spirit. By receiving this grand gift of Love's Salvation, the life of God will permeate in the body. Man is rejuvenated from the inside out and since his mind is on its way to being renewed and transformed, his right thinking follows, then his right living; when man experiences the right living, it will then cause his emotional realm to be calm, collect and comforted. He will now experience an abundant life of contentment that God promises in His Word. Though man will go through trials and tribulation, the love and peace of God will overpower any storm that will arise. God's Word declares in John 16:33, *"These things I have spoken unto you, that in me ye might have peace. In the world ye shall have tribulation: but be of good cheer; I have overcome the world"* (KJV).

Love Inseparable: "Deep Calls to Deep"

It is a love that was from the beginning of time and it is a love that has no end; it is a love that will continue to grow in eternity for the very One Who is the Author of this love. It derives from the Ultimate Creator of the heavens and the earth Who spoke the worlds into existence by His powerful Word. This divine Creator Who is love teaches the soul of man to first receive His genuine love and then, and only then, can this love be given away for others to experience. It is the only true love that heals the despondent personality of the soul, that breaks the shackles to set them free. Although, the need for true love is essential for all of mankind, it is not impossible to attain, for the love of God is shed abroad.

The Hole in the Soul: The Oppressive Distresses

Like the woman with the issue of blood, found in Luke 8:43-48, she experienced a huge hole in her soul. Yes, she had an infirmity in her body, but her issue was deeper. For twelve long years she experienced the emptiness of rejection, loneliness and resentment. Like everyone else, she too searched for the answer for her hurting soul; she longed for a remedy to cure her burdensome distresses[28]. Understand she lived in the time of Jesus where the Levitical Law was very much practiced. This law stated, *"And if a woman have an issue of her blood many days out of the time of her **separation**, or if it run beyond the time of her **separation**; all the days of the issue of her **uncleanness** shall be as the days of her **separation**: she shall be **unclean**. Every bed whereon she lieth all the days of her issue shall be unto her as the bed of her **separation**: and whatsoever she sitteth upon shall be **unclean**, as the **uncleanness** of her **separation** And whosoever toucheth those things shall be **unclean,** and shall wash his clothes, and bathe himself in water, and be unclean until the even. But if she be cleansed of her issue, then she shall number to herself seven days, and after that she shall be clean. And on the eighth day she shall take unto her two turtles, or two young pigeons, and bring them unto the priest, to the door of the tabernacle of the congregation. And the priest shall offer the one for a sin offering, and the other for a burnt offering; and the priest shall make an atonement for her before the* LORD *for the **issue of her uncleanness**. Thus shall ye **separate** the children of Israel from their uncleanness; that they die not in their uncleanness, when they defile my tabernacle that is among them"* (Leviticus 15:25-31, KJV).

It is important to realize that everyone in the community knew she was "unclean" and that she was all alone because of her uncleanness. She was not allowed to touch anything or anyone because by doing so, this would make them unclean as well. For twelve years, if she had children, husband, friends or companions, she could not share the powerful feeling of love's embrace with them. She could not get near to them to whisper the sweet tender words, "I love you" out of fear of perhaps touching them accidentally. Can you imagine the dark separation of her experience due to the heavy yoke of the law upon her shoulders? It was the hefty load of religion and the laden law that kept her bound; until, the day she finally **heard!**

---

[28] The writer refers to this kind of severe situation as, "The Oppressive Distresses" that keep so many, like the woman with the issue of blood, laden and locked in a prison of sorrow.

When speaking about the Pharisees[29] of that time, God's Word declares in Matthew 23:3-5 *"All therefore whatsoever they bid you observe, that observe and do; but do not ye after their works: for they say, and do not. **For they bind heavy burdens** and grievous to be borne, **and lay them on men's shoulders;** but they themselves will not move them with one of their fingers. But all their works they do for to be seen of men: they make broad their phylacteries, and enlarge the borders of their garments"* (KJV). For this reason, she was bound and heavy laden with the ritualistic practices of the parasitical[30] or pharisaical law.

She Heard!!

Due to the heavy load that many experience in their souls, God sent His Word to heal all disease, yes, even in the soul of man. Jesus made a powerful declaration to all the burdensome souls that were heavy laden. He said, *"Come unto me, all ye that labour and are heavy laden, and I will give you rest. **Take my yoke upon you, and learn of me**; for I am meek and lowly in heart: and **ye shall find rest unto your souls"*** (Matthew 11:28-29, KJV). Realize the reason why so many thronged against Jesus as He walked the streets of Galilee. Jesus was a Rabbi[31], but He was not just any ordinary Rabbi, He was a *Semicha* which means, that He was a "Rabbi[32]" with the authority to make his own teaching or interpretation

---

29 The Pharisees were the sect whose name meant, "Separated Ones." These "Separated Ones" observed strict Jewish laws and intolerance to any man or women who was ritually impure.

30 The writer refers to the Pharisees as parasitical, because they drained the life of those who could not possibly keep the law.

31 Like all other rabbis, Jesus had to attend Bet Talmud, which means, "School of Disciples." Between the ages of 12 and 30, there is no mention of Jesus in the Bible; this is because He was attending, Bet Talmud.

32 Author Dwain Miller, author of, Jesus the Rabbi, (Charlotte, NC: LIFEBRIDGE BOOKS, 2013) p. 39, shares information on the meaning of the word, "Rabbi," from author, Brad Young's Jesus the Jewish Theologian, Gospel Research Foundation, Inc., Tulsa, OK. He states, "The title 'Rabbi', in first-century contemporary literature, could refer both to Torah teachers ('Teachers of the Law') and sages, rabbis with Semicha (authority). Jesus, who was clearly recognized by this title, would have fallen into one of these two categories, though clearly—from Scripture—it was the latter."

of the Torah; this was called His Yoke[33]. Dwain Miller, D. Min., author of the book, <u>Jesus the Rabbi</u>, (Charlotte, NC: LIFEBRIDGE BOOKS, 2013) p. 42-43, explains how it was possible for the woman with the issue of blood to hear about the yoke of **Semicha** Jesus. He states:

> "When a rabbi had authority (Semicha), He made his own context of teaching or interpretation of the Torah and it was called his yoke. That is why Jesus said, 'Take My yoke upon you and learn from me…For My yoke is easy and My burden is light' (Matthew 11:29-30).
>
> Jesus was referring to much more than we have understood. He was not simply talking about a team of oxen wearing a heavy yoke, even though it is a picture of religious oppression, He was simply letting the world know that His yoke (interpretation of the law) is easy and His burden is light. You have heard generations of teachings from rabbis telling you could never measure up, but Jesus was declaring that there was a better way to live.
>
> If you ever wondered why Jesus was so popular and could draw crowds of thousands to hear His teachings, the answer is simple: He was a Rabbi with authority (Semicha). The people wrecked all the yokes of the religious leaders of His day because 'He taught them as one having authority, and not as the scribes' (Mark 1:22).
>
> They didn't flock to Him because He could feed them or work miracles. They were hungry, not for food, but for a fresh word from heaven. The people were learning that they could actually have a relationship with God. No longer did they have to feel displaced and unqualified.
>
> Those who were wearing the yoke of religion, were waiting and hoping for someone to lift it from their shoulders. Their whole life they were taught rules and regulations. They knew they didn't qualify and would never be good enough to meet the standards laid down by the religious authorities. They were in a hopeless situation.

---

[33] The "Yoke" refers to the rabbi's method of interpreting the Scripture.

Oppressed by the Romans and condemned by their religion, they were living in a world of darkness.

Like a bolt of lightning, Jesus steps onto the stage of history and declared, 'My yoke is easy, and My burden is light.' Immediately, they knew His teaching was different from the other rabbis. They were hearing things they had never heard before and something stirred in their hearts. Jesus knew that religion was based on fear and guilt, so He didn't step down from heaven to start a new religion! No, a thousand times no! He came to offer a new and better way, and He had the authority (Semicha) to back it up...

...Here was a rabbi who spoke with authority (Semicha) and claimed to be God. The story of His baptism[34] spread like wildfire throughout the land. While they refused to recognize Jesus as the Son of God, they could not deny that He was a rabbi with authority."

This is how the woman with the issue of blood heard[35] about Semicha Jesus who gave her the answer she was always hoping for. Yes, she heard about the grand news naturally because of all the talk and excitement of the new Semicha Who would remove the weight of religion off her back, but moreover she heard[36] with the ears of her heart. She finally understood that her problems began in her soul realm; the struggle that she contended with all along sprang from the

---

[34] At the age of 30, these that graduated from rabbinical school were baptized; the Jewish culture baptized for everything including every process of progression, even in the elementary stages of Bet Talmud. The Baptism was a seal of approval. At this time, Israel was waiting for the next rabbi with Semicha because the two, Hallel and Shamai, who were the Semichas had died. At the Baptism of Jesus is where He received the recognition for Semicha; two witnesses had to testify to the supernatural power of God on a rabbi who was to be a Semicha. The two witnesses were John the Baptist and God the Father.

[35] Mark 5:27 states that she heard of Jesus.

[36] Matthew 13:15 states, *"For this people's heart is waxed gross, and their ears are dull of hearing, and their eyes they have closed; lest at any time they should see with their eyes and **hear with their ears, and should understand with their heart, and should be converted, and I should heal them**"* (KJV).

part that kept her bound. The yoke[37] of her belief that she was not worthy to be loved or embraced had to be broken in order for her spirit man to "hear" the tender loving voice of her Watchman.

As deep calls unto deep, her cry had reached her spirit part, the part of her being where the Spirit of God could inhabit and transform her life. This was the way to her deliverance from her prison of 12 long years. Jesus was the Answer to all of the issues in her soul; she knew now, if she could but touch the hem of His garment, implying that she would definitely take His Yoke, that she would be healed. So as she made her way to Jesus in the crowd; she pressed in to touch the border of His garment, and as soon as she touched Him, her hemorrhaging stopped. As Jesus perceived that virtue had been drawn from Him, He asked, "Who touched Me?" Jesus knew that although there were multitudes of people around Him, that one in particular took from Him the gift of His new interpretation. It was the powerful interpretation of His goodness and grace of the Torah; for He did not do away with the law, but Jesus came to fulfill the law. It was His Powerful Word that would quicken her, making her alive and resurrecting all the other dead things of grief that had caused suffering for so long. And the most profound words that Jesus declared to her that day, are found in Mark 5:34, which states, *"And he said unto her,* **Daughter**, *thy faith hath made thee* **whole***; go in peace, and be* **whole** *of thy plague"* (KJV). This woman, who was now called "daughter," would always have a Heavenly Father to belong to; and, she was not just healed from her flow of blood, she was also made **whole**, which means that every part of her being—her spirit, soul and body, was brought to restoration. This is the very purpose for which God sent His Son to the world; it was for the purpose of drawing the lost and hurting souls back to Himself. It was His *Agape* Love that sent His Son, Jesus, to rescue the lost and the yearning, from the empty hole in their soul.

---

[37] Isaiah 10:27 declares, *"And it shall come to pass in that day, that his burden shall be taken away from off thy shoulder, and his yoke from off thy neck, and the yoke shall be destroyed because of the anointing"* (KJV).

Conclusion

In God's grace and mercy, He always provides a Watchman to whisper in the heart of man to draw nigh to Him. Even in man's sin, the gracious Father is there dealing with his dark heart to persuade him that the choices he continues to make will cause him to fall into a deep pit of regret. Though at times, he almost believes, his soul overrides his spirit and he continues to live in his own vomit of sin. He chooses to please his soul rather than his spirit that longs for a deep inner peace that only can be reached if he accepts the words of the Watchman Who has been with him since the day he was born. He chooses to believe the lies of the deceiver, the very one who persuaded Eve to eat of the Tree of Knowledge of Good and Evil. This schemer of deception was the con artist of the garden who made the forbidden fruit appear more beautiful than it actually was. In the same way, the liar continues to work in the souls of men to keep them bound to the chains of turmoil not intended for God's creation. So, they exist in vomitus- spewed relationships which develop because they have sought a love not from the Spirit of God, but rather it is from the soul realm of man with all its erroneous dwellings. Although, it is a harsh aching they feel, they continue to fill the soul with the mischievous fantasies of the world, perceiving not the answer that goes beyond the soul that will heal the torturous silent section of hell's burning rage that eats away at their insides.

It is the true living God of Christianity, Who is *Agape* Love, Who is the Answer to the yearning soul who hungers for a satisfying peace of mind. He is not an elixir which contains a missing ingredient, or a formula that can be measured by man to get the right amount of solution to cure the ailing heart of grief. There is nothing missing about the Ultimate Creator of the Universe Who does not have to contend with time. He is not a god of religion, a religion in which one must do certain works or penance for salvation, nor is He ritualistic, ceremonial or traditional. He is not a god who employs his power to influence or control the course of lives nor does He work with the accumulation of merits or points in order to gain redemption.

He is the very One Who created man with free-will, with the power to make one's own choice. He is the God of Love who came to save the world and to reconcile with His beloved creation, knowing His children would need help in a corrupt world filled with all kinds of doctrines and religions which will bring ambiguity. He is the God of the certainty of restoration, Who, with anticipation, is ready to win back every man's heart to Himself, within whom He has lovingly embedded His own seed of greatness and purpose. This is the **love** spoken about by the apostles in the Bible that may bring salvation to the displaced soul, if they make a choice to receive His love—the *Agape* Love of God. Until each finds that missing component that completes them, they will always find themselves in a discontented state of mind.

WORKS CITED

Adams, Jay E., <u>Competent to Counsel: Introduction to Nouthetic Counseling</u>, Grand Rapids, Zondervan, 1970

Buscaglia, Ph.D. Leo F., <u>Loving Each Other: The Challenge of Human Relationships</u>, New York, Ballantine, 1984

Carothers, Merlin R., <u>Power in Praise: How the Spiritual Dynamic of Praise Revolutionizes Lives</u>, Escondido, Carothers, 1972

Chapman, Gary, <u>The Five Love Languages: How to Express Heartfelt Commitment to Your Mate</u>, Chicago, Northfield, 1992

Coblentz, Ben, <u>Born to Love: Fifty Meditations on love and loving</u>, Berlin, TGS, 1993

Comfort, Ray, <u>How to Know God Exists: Scientific Proof of God</u>, Alachua, Bridge-Logos, 2007

Cornish, Keith S., "An Atheist's Perspective on Death" *Atheist Foundation of Australia Inc.*, Website: *atheistfoundation.org.au*

Hardy, Luke H., <u>Islam Religion</u>, Lexington, Independent, 2016

Hitchens, Christopher, <u>God is not Great: How Religion Poisons Everything</u>, New York, Twelve Hachette, 2007

Idleman, Kyle, <u>Gods at War: Defeating the Idols that Battle for Your Heart</u>, Grand Rapids, Zondervan, 2013

Jakes, T. D., <u>Intimacy With God: The Spiritual Worship of the Believer</u>, Tulsa, Albury, 2000

—-. Jakes, T. D., <u>The Lady Her Lover, and Her Lord</u>, New York, G. P. Putnam's, 1998

—-. Jakes, T. D., <u>Loved By God: The Spiritual Wealth of the Believer</u>, Tulsa, Albury, 2000

—-. Jakes, T. D., <u>Woman, Thou Art Loosed: Healing the Wounds of the Past</u>, Shippensburg, Treasure, 1993

Kopp, David, Heather, <u>Love Stories God Told: The Great Romances of the Bible</u>, Eugene, Harvest House, 1998

Lewis, C. S., <u>The Four Loves</u>, New York, Houghton, 1960

—-. Lewis, C. S., <u>Mere Christianity</u>, New York, Macmillan, 1943

Meyer, Joyce, <u>Secrets to Exceptional Living: Transforming Your Life through the Fruit of the Spirit</u>, New York, Faith Words, 2002

Mellody, Pia, Wells Andrea, Miller Keith J., <u>Facing Love Addiction: Giving Yourself the Power to Change the Way You Love</u>, New York, Harper, 1992

Miller, Dwain, D. Min., <u>Jesus The Jewish Rabbi</u>, Charlotte, LifeBridge, 2013

Muir, Charles, Caroline, <u>Tantra: The Art of Conscious Loving</u>, San Francisco, Mercury, 1989

Nee, Watchman, <u>The Latent Power of the Soul</u>, New York, Christian Fellowship, 1972

Nicholi, JR., Armand, M., <u>The Question of God: C. S. Lewis and Sigmund Freud Debate God, Love, Sex, and the Meaning of Love</u>, New York, Free, 2002

Piper, John, "God Has Chosen Us in Him Before the Foundation of the Earth: The Conviction Behind this Series" 2013 *Desiring God Foundation. Website: desiringGod.org*

Prochnik, George, <u>Putnam Camp: Sigmund Freud, James Putnam, and the Purpose of American Psychology</u>, New York, Other Press, 2006

Rao, Chaya, <u>Buddhist</u>, Middletown, LCPublisfish, 2014

Shakespeare, William, *Romeo and Juliet*, Act II, Scene 2

Sumrall, Lester, <u>The Names of God: God's Character revealed through His Names</u>, New Kensington, Whitaker, 1982

—-. Sumrall, Lester, <u>Spirit Soul & Body: Bring Wholeness and Joy into Your Life</u>, New Kensington, Whitaker, 1984

Tallis, Frank, "Crazy for You" The *Psychologist*. London: February 2005. Vol. 18, No 2.

Vroom, Hendrik M., <u>Religions and the Truth: Philosophical Reflections and Perspectives</u>, Grand Rapids, EERDMANS, 1989

ABOUT THE AUTHOR

 Dr. Monica Martinez, ThD, and her husband, Dr. Paul Martinez, are the pastors of the congregation Greater Faith Church in Corpus Christi, Texas. They have been pastoring for twenty years now. Pastor Monica has been a licensed minister of the State of Texas since 1993 and was ordained a minister of the gospel in 2003. She faithfully ministered ten years as a volunteer chaplain in the Nueces County Jail (Clergy). She holds an Associate in Arts Psychology Degree (Del Mar College); Bachelor of Arts in Biblical Studies and Theology with honors (Corpus Christi Theological Seminary); Master of Arts in Biblical Studies and Theology with honors, cum laude (Minnesota Graduate School of Theology); Doctor of Theology with honors, cum laude (Minnesota Graduate School of Theology); and is a permanent member of the dean's list from South Texas Bible Institute. She continues to labor in the love of God alongside her husband in pursuing the vision that God has imparted into their lives in making disciples of Christ in the Coastal Bend area. This vision is established and confirmed in the gospel according to Matthew 28:19, which declares, "Therefore go and make disciples of all nations, baptizing them in the name of the Father and of the Son and of the Holy Spirit." (NIV).

www.ingramcontent.com/pod-product-compliance
Lightning Source LLC
Chambersburg PA
CBHW060336130626
46553CB00003B/1022